NO LONGER A
SECRET

NO LONGER A
SECRET

The church and
violence
against women

Aruna Gnanadason

Risk
BOOK SERIES

WCC Publications, Geneva

Cover design: Rob Lucas
Cover picture: Rob Lucas
Cover p. 4 photo: WCC/Peter Williams

ISBN 2-8254-1098-5

No. 58 in the Risk book series

Printed in Switzerland

Dedicated to

Mercy, my mother

and

Joy, my mother-in-law

Two women who gave me life and taught me courage,
each in her own way.

Table of Contents

1. Facing the Reality

"Go back to him... learn how to adjust to his moods... don't do anything that would provoke his anger... Christ suffered and died for you on the Cross... Can't you bear some suffering too?"

This is a voice of the church — the words of a priest counselling a woman who was being battered by her husband every single day of her married life. She went to the church for refuge and for moral and spiritual support. What she received instead was advice to learn submissiveness and obedience in a distorted relationship and an abusive marriage.

The response to women's cries for justice and fair treatment is not always so heartless. There are occasions when women have experienced the caring concern of a community of Christians. There are exceptional examples of radical actions of solidarity taken by the church. But by and large, the churches around the world have remained silent about violence against women. Too often it is treated as a marginal concern, relegated to the attention of *women* in the church, not recognized as an issue central to the church's life and witness because of its deep and dehumanizing effects on the lives of women in the community.

When women live in violent contexts or in constant fear it has a deleterious effect on the development of societies as a whole. Unfortunately, this is not taken as seriously as it should be by either the church or other institutions in society. MATCH, a Canadian nongovernmental organization, concludes that:

> Violent acts against women the world over attack their dignity as human beings and leave them vulnerable and fearful. Conditioned to undervalue their skills and abilities and paralyzed by real fears of violence and retribution, women are marginalized in society and forced out of decision-making processes which shape and determine the development of their communities. [1]

Women have to be able to participate fully in their country's plans, policies and programmes if development is to take place. As long as they are stifled in their participation by fear of violence, as long as they are reluctant to take up leadership positions because they are subject to physical or emotional abuse, the progress of whole populations will suffer.

It is the denial of this truth and the church's failure to offer adequate support or a concerted response that have prompted women around the world to raise the issue of violence against them as a priority area on the agenda of the Ecumenical Decade of the Churches in Solidarity with Women (1988-1998). With alarming consistency, women from all regions of the world are identifying the various forms of violence they live with and calling on the church to respond.

Identifying the forms of violence

It should be recognized that women have begun to speak out their pain only in recent times. For centuries, violence against women has been one of the world's best kept secrets. Even today, published statistics from around the world on crimes against women do not reflect the full picture since they refer only to *reported* incidents of violence. Within the very male-dominated contexts of all societies, much violence against women goes unreported. Moreover, at every stage — from the family to the church to the police to the law courts — the understanding of "violence" excludes or ignores many forms of emotional, psychological and physical abuse that women experience.

No region or country is exempt from expressions of violence against women. Statistics collected by the New York-based International Women's Tribune Centre from women around the world are staggering, to say the least.[2]
— In Costa Rica, one of every two women can expect to be a victim of violence at some point in her life.
— In Jamaica, where rape is not a criminal offence, 1088 cases of rape and carnal abuse were reported in 1989.

— In Canada, one in four women can expect to be assaulted at some point in their lives, half of these before the age of 17.

— According to UN reports, India leads the world in "custodial" rape (rape committed by men in positions of power such as police officers, prison and hospital staff, doctors).

— In the US, a woman is beaten every 15 seconds; every six minutes a rape occurs; every day four women are killed by their batterers.

— A report by the Mexican Federation of Women's Trade Unions says that 95 percent of Mexican women workers are victims of sexual harassment in their workplaces.

— Three-quarters of the women interviewed in an International Labour Office (ILO) study of plantation workers in Sri Lanka said they had been beaten by their husbands or estate superintendents.

— In the Philippines, one out of every two women arrested by the military is forced to undress, according to a study on rape by the military. Fourteen percent reported that they were slapped, boxed or severely mauled; another 14 percent were harassed and threatened with rape or death.

— In Peru, one of every four girl children will be the victim of sexual abuse before she reaches her sixteenth birthday, and a third of all adult women report that they have been forced to have sex against their will.

Many other sources provide evidence of equally horrifying proportions. *African Woman* tells the story of eleven women who were raped by soldiers in April 1991 while they were being held with thousands of other civilians in Uganda for identity checks and questioning.[3] The picture is clear: all over the world women are being brutalized and violated.

Recent research points to an even more frightening trend: women belong to an "endangered species". On the basis of demographic statistics from around the world, Harvard economist Amartya Sen estimates that the number of females "missing" due to biases against them could well be over 100 million. One reason for this shortfall is that girls are not allowed to benefit as much as boys from improvements in health care and nutrition that are lowering death rates. Under normal circumstances, from 5 to 6 percent more boys than girls are born; and at every age thereafter males die at higher rates than females. In the US, Britain and Poland, for example, there are about 105 females to every 100 males. In India, by contrast, the 1991 census showed that there are only 92.9 females to every 100 males, down from 93.4 in 1981. The 1990 census in China found just 93.8 females to every 100 males, compared with 94.1 at the time of the 1982 census. These and similar statistics from Afghanistan, Bangladesh, Bhutan, Nepal, Pakistan, Papua New Guinea and Turkey found in the United Nations 1991 report on "The World's Women" confirm that in many countries, the ratio between women and men is decreasing.[4] This form of violence against women cannot be ignored.

The roots of the problem

It is necessary to unearth the roots of the violence to which women are exposed if we are to combat it effectively. In recent years, women have used the term "patriarchy" to articulate one understanding of existing unequal power relations in the world, and to describe the violence that women face in their homes, in the workplace and elsewhere in society. Such violence is seen as an expression of the wider violent and militarized context of the world in which we live. Patriarchy is identified as a system of "graded subjugation" in which some have power over others. This power can be manifested in economic, political, social or cultural terms.

The new definition, which goes beyond how the church has traditionally understood the term "patriarchy", underscores the fact that men in all societies have an unfair edge over women. It is true that it is not only women who live in violence but all people on the fringes of society — men, women and children, the "little ones" of this world, who live without power under the shadow of death-dealing forces. But in all contexts, women are the primary victims.

Crisis points in the world manifest the general culture of violence and militarism pervading political, economic, social and cultural life in every region. Global economic and social structures create the atmosphere for unequal power relations between and within nations. This engineers inequalities and keeps intact the atmosphere of violence of which women are special targets.

In every society, they are the most vulnerable and, along with children, the ones who bear the brunt of the world's injustice. Their sexuality is exploited, as is evident from the image of women projected in the media. Their labour is exploited, and any crisis in the economic structure hits women first. Women in the South suffer tremendous hardship working long hours in unhealthy and and unhygienic surroundings. They eke out a living in squatter settlements and slums and as the rural poor, lacking basic amenities, nutrition, health care, maternity and child care facilities. Women have always been viewed as a reserve army of cheap and docile labour. The recession and cutbacks on social welfare spending affect the lives of women in the North as well, particularly single mothers, migrants and refugee women and workers in poorly paid jobs. There is no doubt that in all our societies, women are the poorest of the poor and the most economically marginalized, unfairly burdened by the current global economic crisis.

What is even more insidious is that the violence women experience is considered to be secondary to the other forms of violence prevalent in the world. But it cannot be denied that "sexism kills". According to the well-known crusader against gender violence, Charlotte Bunch, "there is increasing documentation of the many ways in which being female is life-threatening," and a woman is unsafe at every stage of life, even before she is born.[5]

Bunch provides a number of examples to illustrate her point. *Before birth*, the medical procedure of amniocentesis continues to be used solely to determine the sex of the foetus, leading to widespread abortion of female foetuses, particularly in China and India, where more males than females are born even though natural birth ratios would produce more females. *During childhood*, the World Health Organization (WHO) reports, girls in many countries are fed less, breast-fed for shorter periods of time, taken to doctors less frequently than boys. As a result, girls are physically and mentally maimed by malnutrition or die at higher rates than boys. *In adulthood*, Bunch says, the denial of women's right to control their reproductive capacities threatens their lives, especially where it is combined with poverty and poor health services.

It is thus evident that the increased incidence of such violence against women as wife-beating, rape and dowry deaths cannot be dealt with as only crime statistics or dismissed as individual aberrations of demented males (though there are frequent examples of men who are passing through some deep psychological crisis going on a rampage of violence against women). Most incidents of violence are manifestations of social structures that perpetuate personal and systemic injustice.

Whatever its form, violence has its roots in distorted power relations. Patriarchal violence has not been adequately understood nor acknowledged as a necessary framework for analyzing structural inequalities in society. Yet unless there is a shift in the way unequal power relations are defined and a challenge to concepts that legitimize the imbalance of power in the hands of a few, who are largely males, there is no way to tackle the systemic roots of the violence against women, nor to respond adequately to individual incidents. This still remains an open challenge.

Women have attributed the increased violence of the past two decades to a "backlash" against the women's movement. There has been resistance to the organized voices of women and their determination to speak out against all that oppresses them, and serious attempts to undermine women's struggles for basic human rights. One way in which this is done is to develop a sophisticated methodology of control, including the use of force, to "teach women a lesson" so that they will know better than to rebel or question their status and position.

Violence in the lives of women may take blatant forms. Or it may be subtle. In either case, it eats into women's psyches, demoralizing them and lowering their self-esteem. To categorize the specific forms of violence women face as "overt" or "covert" is not to imply that there are some forms of violence which are "private" and therefore can be resisted in an isolated manner. All violence against women has systemic roots. The categories described below are not rigid, because they are interrelated. Nor is the list exhaustive; it is rather an attempt to identify and describe some expressions of violence.

Overt forms of violence

Violence in the domestic sphere

In the past, it was often virtually impossible to know what happened inside the family home, but since women have dared to speak out their pain, this information is no longer secret. Even so, statistics on crime in the public sphere attract more attention than figures on violence in the home. People tend to fear danger in the streets and lament and condemn rising crime rates in society, but often ignore the reality of abuse in the home.

As the truth about domestic violence is revealed, it is becoming indisputable that women and children are not necessarily safe even in the apparent security of their homes. In many contexts all over the world the family, far from being a place where men, women and children live in an atmosphere of shared understanding, respect and love, has supported patriarchal forms of domination and power. The culture of patriarchal domination and violent retribution against any expression of what the dominant person considers rebellion or dissent finds expression in various forms of physical and sexual abuse of women by men in their homes in all societies and among all peoples.

In a bid to preserve the myth that the family is and always will be a safe unit within the community, many people prefer not to pay attention to the startling details of violence in the family now emerging.

In many societies, it is considered "normal" if a man beats his wife, even by most medical health professionals. However, if a woman dares to retaliate with violence she is treated as "mentally abnormal". Only recently have medical professionals recognized the existence of the "battered wife syndrome", a term coined by a US psychologist in 1984 to explain the behaviour of abused victims.

Tolerance of domestic violence manifests itself in warped cultural practices and attitudes. There is an old Hindi saying: "A woman is like spit. Once spat out, she cannot be taken back." In many Asian societies, a woman is conditioned from the moment she is born into accepting that her only purpose in life is to be married and to stay married at all costs. This implies submissiveness to a man no matter how cruel or violent he may be. Most societies have similar written or unwritten expectations of women.

For social workers, lawyers and counsellors trying to deal with domestic violence, one of its most perplexing and difficult features is the inability of many abused women to make a break from their violent home environment because they are bound by strong emotional ties to the abuser. Studies show that battered women tend to return to a violent relationship many times over before leaving for good and making their lives in a safe environment. In many cases, a woman is unable to name the violence in her life. Maybe she is too proud to acknowledge that her marriage is not working. Maybe she is hoping against hope that the repeated promises her husband makes to desist from violence will be kept.

Domestic violence takes many forms, including intimidation and threats, economic deprivation, psychological and sexual abuse, often used repeatedly. Physical violence is one tactic used. It may take the form of a single attack, but is often frequent and in some cases even daily. The assumption that such violence happens only among poor and uneducated people or in "dysfunctional" families is a myth. Studies show that a man who regularly batters his wife or partner and children may be a perfect "gentleman" outside the home. He may be a doctor, minister, lawyer, psychologist, teacher or other professional who would never be violent to other men or women in the public sphere. He can control himself outside, but picks a safe target inside the home.

In no context do women "ask" to be beaten or abused. It should be added that in over 95 percent of domestic assaults, the man is the assailant. There are rare cases in which a woman batters a man, and women have been known to retaliate and sometimes even kill their attacker after prolonged years of battering. But violence in the home is overwhelmingly by men against women.

Statistics are available in plenty:

— In South Africa, one adult woman out of every six is assaulted regularly by her mate. In almost half of these cases, the man involved also abuses the woman's children.

— In France, 95 percent of the victims of violence are women, 51 percent of them at the hands of their husbands.

— In Papua New Guinea, 60 percent of the persons murdered in 1981 were women, the majority by their spouses during or after a domestic argument.
— In the USA, violence occurs at least once in 67 percent of all marriages.
— In cases of sexual abuse of children in Canada, most assailants are either family members or persons in a position of trust, according to a 1981 survey. [6]

In most societies, the demands of new economic and social realities are changing the role expectations of both men and women. Nevertheless, some old patterns are not easy to get rid of. Even women who have full-time paid jobs outside of the home are expected in most contexts to depend on men socially and economically, while men continue to be dependent on women for domestic services, including a kind of psycho-emotional support sometimes referred to as "tension management". It continues to be the woman's responsibility to create a home atmosphere that will help men to deal with the pressures of the workplace.

As a Canadian church report notes:

> The role of tension manager is the domestic task that leaves a woman most vulnerable to violence from her male partner. In fact, violence against women can be seen as an extreme form of tension management in which a woman absorbs with her body and soul tensions generated in the public sphere — tensions which could otherwise be directed in protest against oppression from the established order. [7]

Sexual harassment

Like rape, sexual harassment has been a hidden problem, treated as a joke or blamed on the victim herself. Because of a long history of silence on the subject, many women feel uncomfortable, embarrassed or ashamed when they talk of personal incidents of harassment. They are afraid that it will reflect badly on their character or that they will be seen as somehow inviting the propositions. [8]

A clear and comprehensive definition of sexual harassment has been provided by the General Assembly of the United Presbyterian Church in the USA. It refers to "any unwanted sexual advance or demands (verbal/physical) which are perceived by the recipient as demeaning, intimidating or coercive". Sexual contact that is *unwanted* in the *perception of the recipient* is therefore to be treated as sexual harassment. The need for a more accurate definition of what constitutes sexual harassment arises from the fact that in many countries, the law courts have been ambivalent about it. Only recently has sexual harassment come to be recognized as a form of violence.

In the past, women did not have the courage to challenge the daily irritation experienced at the hands of people with authority over them, particularly in the workplace. Nor would they have defined this as sexual harassment. But due to the impact of the women's movement, more and more women in many societies now refuse to be treated as objects. Recognizing how much it affects their humanity and dignity, they are no longer able to accept harassment without protest.

But it is also true that most women would still prefer to cultivate an immune system that makes them apparently indifferent to any assault on their sensibilities — verbal, psychological or physical. The motto continues to be: pretend nothing happened rather than go through a process that could cause a great deal of personal agony. Women are not sure that they will be believed if they complain of sexual harassment. They may be ridiculed for being prudish or oversensitive, or even blamed for provoking unwanted behaviour. The consequences on their private lives and family situations can be devastating. In most cases, they would rather not speak out because to do so may cost them their jobs. In most societies, laws to protect women are far from adequate. It is difficult to prove that a woman's modesty and psyche have been wounded by inappropriate words or actions.

The preliminary findings of a 1992 research project instituted by the Swiss government office for equality between women and men confirms just how widespread the problem is. The survey included a detailed interview of 558 women working in 25 different companies and agencies in Geneva. Of the women interrogated, 59 percent affirmed that they had been sexually harrassed at work in the preceding two years. Seventy-one percent of these said the harassment had occurred more than once, and 87 percent of those said the same man had harassed them.

Among the causes for complaint were inappropriate comments about women (35 percent), colleagues' attitudes which caused embarrassment (30 percent), ambiguous or embarrassing comments (19 percent), colleagues showing them pornographic material or leaving it out on display (16 percent), unwanted touching (14 percent), sexual blackmail (2 percent), imposed sexual relations (0.7 percent), physical violence (0.4 percent), and rape or attempted rape (0.2 percent). For 81 percent of the women who experienced sexual harassment, the disagreeable situation lasted for more than a year; of these 16 percent complained of daily harassment for more than a year.

Sexual harassment and fear of it exert social control on women. Research has revealed that women unable to act or behave as they wish adopt "self-censuring" behaviour. Women in all situations impose restrictions of time, space, and movement on themselves because they must always be on guard. At the same time, the non-recognition of sexual harassment as a social reality contributes to the maintenance of silence on the subject. The effect is to lead women to believe that sexual harassment is an integral and inevitable part of their work conditions.[9]

Trade unions have not yet been able to deal with incidents of sexual harassment as "crimes against working women", although many studies have shown that the majority of working women experience some degree of harassment at some stage of their working lives. A few years ago, a group of women brought a case of harassment to the attention of the leading trade union in a nationalized bank in Bangalore, India: a man had slapped a woman colleague at work. The union declined to take up the case, saying it was a personal matter between the woman and man concerned and needed to be dealt with in that way.

An International Labour Office (ILO) report on sexual harassment shows just how widespread and global the problem is. But ILO civil rights lawyer Constance Thomas admits that the attempt to examine the scope of sexual harassment in third-world worksites has only now begun. "We think we are going to find an even more serious problem there," she acknowledged. [10]

Rape

The issue of rape has recently received increased attention in connection with its incidence in wars and conflict situations. The use of women's bodies as weapons in conflict causes revulsion in the minds of all right-thinking people. What it does to the psyche of women who are its victims can never be fully understood or adequately responded to. But despite this awareness of the deep wounds caused, there are still attempts to underestimate or deny the seriousness of this crime. As a brochure from a feminist group in Bangalore, India, points out:

> Rape, which is the most aggressive demonstration of unjust power relationships, as a form of personal violence, is physical assault and symbolic of the degradation of womankind, but is a violation of the most sensitive part of the female psyche. Susan Brownmiller defines it as a "conscious process of intimidation by which all men keep all women in a state of fear". It is only of late that rape is being viewed as a criminal attack against an individual and specifically a woman. Otherwise, the shocking sentiment implicit even today in the law, besides the attitude of society, is that a woman "asks for it", or in a spirit of condonation states that a rapist is an individual giving in to his natural virility! [11]

Old assumptions and attitudes die hard. Some years ago, the chief minister of an Indian state complained that the media were blowing attacks on women tourists out of proportion. "What is rape after all?" he asked at a public meeting, adding: "In America a rape occurs every minute. It is as common as drinking tea. One drinks tea and commits a rape."[12]

In July 1991, 271 teenage girls were attacked by male classmates at a boarding school in Kenya because they refused to join a strike against the school authorities. Nineteen girls died of suffocation as they tried to hide, and 71 were raped. The comment by the school's deputy principal was revealing: "The boys never meant any harm against the girls," he asserted. "They just wanted to rape." The editor of Kenya's *Weekly Review*, however, condemned the incident:

> The tragedy has underscored the abominable male chauvinism that dominates Kenyan social life. The lot of our women and girls is lamentable. We treat them as second-class beings, good only for sexual gratification or burdensome chores. We bring up our boys to have little or no respect for girls.[13]

Attitudes such as that of the Indian government minister, the Kenyan educator or the man who shot dead 14 young women at the University of Montreal in 1989 because, he said, they were feminists, may be extreme and isolated reactions, but they unfortunately reflect some old and universal assumptions and attitudes. No real change will be achieved unless these are exposed and radically changed. In many countries, law courts have excused perpetrators of crimes against women on the grounds of the woman's past history. From logic it follows that there are some women who can never be raped!

Rape as a weapon of war

The most brutal part of the build-up of private methods of control to repress people's protest movements in many societies is the increasing incidence of sexual violence against women. Newspaper reports of war and other conflict situations, police action or military intervention often include the phrase "and many women were raped". Mass rape has frequently been used as a political or military weapon either to punish or to intimidate those who rebel. The logic here is to hurt the women in order to teach the men a lesson.

More than forty years after World War II, hundreds of women in Korea, the Philippines and other countries are speaking out about the systematic abuse they experienced at the hands of Japanese soldiers during the war. These women were kidnapped and used as "comfort women" for the soldiers' pleasure. Only now have they finally asserted their right to protest that deep humiliation and to demand financial compensation. But, as a Dutch woman testifying in 1992 to the UN Commission on Human Rights in Geneva said, the deep and lasting psychological damage sustained can never really be compensated for or erased. Courageous enough to speak out as one of the victims of this forced prostitution, the woman concluded her statement by asserting that "I have the right, after almost 50 years, not to forgive all those who caused all the pain."

Rape has often been considered as a "normal by-product" of war. An *International Herald Tribune* editorial (8 December 1992) put it starkly: "All wars are alike in at least three particulars: death, destruction and rape." The comment points to the matter-of-fact attitude with which brutality against women in any conflict situation is viewed.

This hard reality hit the world with fresh force in reports emerging in 1992 from the war in the former Yugoslavia. Rape as an inevitable part of the war was openly acknowledged by all sides in the conflict. The *International Herald Tribune* editorial mentioned above, aptly titled "The rape of Bosnia", was written in that context. It quotes a *New York Times* interview with a Serbian fighter, who explained that his commanders had advised him and his companions that raping Muslim women was "good for raising a fighter's morale", and that he had followed their advice several times at a motel used as a prison for Muslim women. He also claimed that he and his fellow fighters routinely killed the women afterwards.

Ecumenical teams of women who visited the former Yugoslavia in 1992 confirmed the veracity of such accounts, as did delegations from the European Community, Amnesty International and the UN Human Rights Commission. Evidence of systematic mass rape as part of the military strategy there was picked up by the media and caused consternation around the world. Not all the raped women were killed, however. Many survived and went to refugee camps around the divided country, and a few were able to tell the world of their pain. In the framework of the "ethnic cleansing" strategy, some had been detained for at least five months after being made pregnant, by which time abortion was illegal. New expressions like "frontline" and "third-party rape", describing public rape as a means of intimidating and demoralizing enemy forces, have been added to the jargon of warfare. Like other weapons, rape too is becoming more sophisticated!

Article 27, paragraph 2 of the Fourth Geneva Convention on the Protection of Civilian Persons in Times of War (adopted in 1949) classifies wartime rape as a serious human rights violation. It states that "women shall be especially protected against any attack on their honour, in particular against rape, enforced prostitution, or any form of indecent assault." In an agreement reached under the auspices of the International Red Cross, all parties in the Yugoslavia conflict undertook to comply with the Convention. Yet the law has been flouted with impunity. Women are demanding the implementation of the Fourth Geneva Convention in order to ensure that rape is considered a war crime. Women who are dehumanized and violated in this and other wars cannot wait another forty years before justice is done!

Amnesty International reports the rape of political prisoners and women imprisoned in conflict situations in India, the Philippines, Bangladesh, Pakistan, Liberia, Mauritius, Uganda, Senegal, Peru, Guatemala, Mexico, Turkey, Greece, Ireland, and Palestine. The report stipulates that:

> Through their failure to institute adequate investigations, prosecutions and procedural safeguards, governments around the world bear full responsibility for the persistence of widespread rape and sexual abuse in custody. Women are entitled to the protection of their fundamental human rights. But many governments clearly regard rape and sexual assault as less serious offences than other human rights violations. This is a particularly frightening prospect when the perpetrators of these rapes are the same policemen and military personnel charged with the protection of the public. [14]

Prostitution

Prostitution, particularly related to tourism, is now being recognized not only as a grave affront to women's being and psyche but also as a form of violence against women. Poor women tend to be the victims of its most ugly and dehumanizing manifestations. The link between prostitution and global economic injustice and the market economy is increasingly recognized, and it was recently said that a poor nation's most marketable commodity is its women, although statistics show that it is now *children* — the most fragile, unorganized and thus exploitable human beings — who are the main targets of prostitution. Writes Jean Fernand-Laurent, the rapporteur of a 1983 UN Economic and Social Council study on the sex trade:

> The movement involves the traffic of poor women towards rich men in all directions. Economic structural adjustment and loan repayments are causing much anguish to

people in the South. Thirty-seven percent of the Philippines annual budget flows from the country to service debts, while poverty is such that 21,000 women work as prostitutes around the US Subic naval base. In situations of poverty, women and children are the first to suffer, and therefore also to seek desperate survival strategies. The sex industry has rapidly become international, profiting from this vulnerability.[15]

In Belgium, for example, an estimated 2000 women are illegally employed in cabarets, and their numbers are rising each year. Of the 1430 work permits granted to "artistes" in Flanders in 1990, 968 were for "go-go" dancers, of whom 290 were from the Dominican Republic, 228 from the Philippines, 77 from Thailand, 42 from Brazil, 34 from Romania, and 30 from the former USSR. Social workers estimate that 30-50 percent of prostitutes in Belgium are non-Europeans. Sex tourism is the flip side of the coin: each year, 10,000 Belgian men travel as sex tourists to Pattaya in Thailand.

A study commissioned by the German government ministry for women shows that of the 222,000 German tourists who travelled to Thailand in 1989, seven out of ten were men and between 50 and 70 percent of them were travelling to Thailand exclusively for sex purposes.

Although prostitution is treated as a crime for foreign women in Germany, roughly half of the country's 2-400,000 prostitutes, in the big cities at least, are non-Germans. Previously they came mainly from Thailand but, over the last three years, more Latin American women have been working as prostitutes in Frankfurt, while women from Poland, the former Czechoslovakia and Hungary are doing likewise in Hamburg and Berlin.

Many of the estimated 20,000 prostitutes in the Netherlands are also foreign women. The Dutch government is developing new policy guidelines on the sex industry and has set up a support centre called the Stichting Tegen Vrouwenhandel (STV). Of the 168 women aged from 16-39 who contacted the centre between 1989 and 1991, 47 were Dominicans, 38 Filipinas, 37 from Thailand, 9 from Poland, Bulgaria and Yugoslavia.

A "Frauen Informationszentrum", an organization working with prostitutes and abused women in Switzerland, counselled 132 women in 1990. Of these 32 were from Brazil, 29 from the Dominican Republic, 25 from Thailand, 7 from Kenya, 6 from the Philippines. Women also came from as far afield as Eritrea, Mozambique, Tahiti, Uganda, Cuba and Colombia. A 1991 study estimates that each year, 25-30,000 Swiss men travelling abroad will indulge in sexual relations with child prostitutes.

Child prostitution is on the increase all over the world. There are estimated to be up to several hundreds of thousands of prostitutes under the age of 16 in Thailand, for example. [16] In many parts of the world, child prostitutes are drawn mainly from indigenous populations. Nearly one-third of the child prostitutes in Taiwan, for instance, are from indigenous communities despite the fact that only 2 percent of the total population are indigenous. [17]

A letter from a Thai child prostitute expresses the pain of millions of girl children being inducted into the sex trade every day:

Dear Daddy and Mom,
I write to you because I miss you... I am not working as a servant, but as a prostitute. Each day I must serve 7-8 men. I can get diseases like VD, TB, AIDS, etc. They threaten to beat me up if I don't do it. They beat up girls who refused them, until they died. They won't take us to be treated because they are afraid that we will run away. Instead they give us two or three tablets... Being a prostitute is like being a bird in a cage. They can't fly away. [18]

Mail-order brides
These are women from poorer nations who are sold as brides, to men in Europe and Australia in particular. The

practice is now being recognized as a new form of violence against women. Women from the South are advertised as "exotic, graceful, beautiful, loyal, reliable," but also "submissive, good with children, not too independent, from a socially stable environment, morally old-fashioned but with a modern outlook, and protected with a health certificate"! Describing its "merchandise", a British marriage bureau promised that "in selecting a Filipina, you could expect her to be passionate yet faithful, loving and caring, hard-working and with none of the hangups in attitudes prevalent in European women."[19]

In 1987, some 200 German agencies were advertising mail-order brides.[20] Marriage bureaus make use of the three-month tourist visa to bring women picked from a catalogue to Germany. Several agencies then offer a "trial period" before a final decision is reached! Prices vary considerably depending on the woman's country of origin. Central and eastern European women are available at the cheapest rate. A Munich agency charges 3500 marks to make contact with a woman from Hungary, Bulgaria or the former Czechoslovakia, and includes her travel costs. If the client does not want to marry her within six months, 50 percent of the fee is returned.

Swiss agencies also offer mail-order bride services and men may also return the women should they prove "unsuitable". It costs between 5-7000 Swiss francs — what one would pay for a good second-hand car — to order a wife from the Philippines. Half of the 28 mail-order brides who sought counsel at the Frauen Informationszentrum in 1989 were being subjected to violence and abuse. Of these 22 had to be treated for injuries resulting from beatings, and had been sexually abused and/or raped.

Other forms of violence that deeply affect the well-being and even survival of women in different contexts are being identified. Among them are some medical techniques, including the invasive power of reproductive technologies, the sex-specific torture of women prisoners, violent attacks on female political and human rights activists, incest and other forms of child abuse including female infanticide, dowry-related violence and even murder, cultural practices like female circumcision and self-immolation by widows, ritual abuse particularly of girl children and the continuing practice of witch-hunting, distorted images of women in the media, advertising and pornography, gang rapes and rape in marriage. Women of colour and other women exposed to rising racial hatred and discrimination are the particular targets of violence. In a recent interview, Dalit women's activist Ruth Manorama said that more than 80 percent of women raped in India are from this oppressed community.

Covert forms of violence

There are more subtle and elusive forms of violence against women that cannot be counted in hard statistics. These include the living deaths millions of women face in their homes, workplaces and other social contexts where they are subjected to discriminatory and dehumanizing attitudes to them *as* women. Such attitudes may be expressed in cruel taunts and harassment that devalue women, denying their right to an opinion, suppressing their desires, locking them into the drudgery of domestic labour, and diminishing their creativity and self-esteem.

Such covert violence is rarely taken seriously. Women are advised not to "over-react" to what are considered "normal" attitudes and to behaviour that is sometimes said to be unconscious and not intended to cause discomfort or pain. But some women are asserting that any form of violence, be it verbal, psychological, emotional or physical, is dehumanizing and therefore unacceptable. They recognize that any attitude or behaviour that reduces women to the level of targets of abuse or harassment is violence. They are demanding that *all* forms of violence from the most blatant to the most subtle be challenged and combatted. Around the world, the women's movement has given them the courage and the space to articulate a vision of life free from violence, where all may contribute, and everyone's gifts may be respected and allowed to flourish.

2. No Longer Silent

My comrade
Just a minute!
Before you strike my cheek with your uplifted hand,
Just think for a minute!

Was your hand lifted
Against the industrialist
Who sucked your life out
Making you work for more than eight hours a day
For a pittance?
No, it wasn't!

Was your hand lifted
Against the politician/leader
Who made a thousand promises
During all the past election campaigns
But quickly forgot you and his promises?
No, it wasn't!

But you lift your hand against me
Just because a cup of coffee has gone cold!

You, who allowed your humanity to be trampled on
So as to ensure your next meal,
You who allowed your humanity
To be debased.
Are you going to debase my humanity
Just for a cup of coffee?

My comrade,
Before you strike my cheek
With your uplifted hand,
Just think for a minute!

Subadhra
(Translated from the original Tamil)

Subadhra's voice expresses women's efforts to reclaim their right to violence-free lives. All over the world, women are recognizing that for too long they have remained silent while their bodies and souls have been the innocent targets of violence and are saying: "Enough is enough!" All over the world such expressions of courage and resistance offer signs of hope.

A few years ago, I met a newly-married woman who was being battered by her husband on just about any pretext. When she told her mother and grandmother about the agony she was going through, they advised her to go back to her husband and learn to tolerate his violence. "All these years, your father and grandfather ill-treated us too," they said. "We took it silently. You too must learn how to accept this. It's our fate for having been born women." Luckily, this young woman was aware that there were other options open to her. She was convinced that she could live alone and take care of herself and therefore did not have to continue submitting to humiliation and violence. After many attempts to heal her marriage, she reluctantly but firmly opted out of the abusive relationship. But millions of women around the world stay imprisoned in painful and sometimes even dangerous home environments.

Over the past two decades, the women's movement has brought into sharp focus the various dimensions and extent of the violence women experience in society, the workplace and the public domain as well as in the supposedly safe setting of their homes. The truth revealed has empowered other women to recognize that they need not bear silently the blows of a dehumanized society that systematically condones and even legitimizes violence. The movement has created a space and climate in which women can tell their stories of physical and mental intimidation and express their pain.

Women have devised various ways to create a secure world for themselves. Subadhra, whose poem I quoted above, and thousands of women like her use poetry, song, drama and street theatre and other creative media to get their message across. In every region of the world, audiovisuals, comic books and simple booklets have been produced as educational tools to help women teach their sisters to protest, resist and protect themselves against increasing violence.

Educational materials like those prepared by the Nicaraguan Association of Rural Workers are an example of such work. Since 1983, the association has made awareness-raising on women's rights among its members, both male and female, one of its principal goals. Using pictures of typical work and family situations, women farmworkers teach small groups of men and women to reflect on their lives. Issues discussed include sexual harassment in the workplace and physical and psychological abuse in the home.

A Namibian group concerned by rising crime rates against women runs workshops and training programmes to improve legal knowledge and organizing skills so that women may be prepared to deal with violence. The project includes neighbourhood women's support groups to ensure that women are trained to understand the social mechanisms creating violence, and learn to develop strategies to deal with it.

The "All Women's Action Movement" (AWAM) in Kuala Lumpur, Malaysia, has helped raise public awareness on the extent of domestic and other forms of violence against women in Malaysian society. Their action pack on legal reforms includes illustrated stories of women who have sought refuge or legal redress, a list of state legal offices to which women may turn, and examples of constructive action by victims and their support groups.

Posters on billboards across the city, in buses and trams, plus a city-wide mailing were part of a massive educational campaign on rape organized in Geneva, Switzerland, by "Viol Secours", a rape crisis centre, in 1992. The campaign message was simple: "Silent acceptance or resistance? How are *you* going to respond to sexual violence?" The telephone number and address of the shelter was supplied. Primarily, the campaign offered a helping hand to women threatened by violence (who are often unable to escape because they do not know whom to trust or depend on). But the campaign message was also addressed to all women as well as to men.

A "Women and Law" committee in Papua New Guinea has done intensive educational work on the issue of domestic violence. PNG statistics are alarming: 43 percent of people killed by violence in 1979 were women; by 1981 the figure had risen to 61 percent. The committee distributed thousands of leaflets and posters explaining that wife-beating is against the law, and produced a television video for people who cannot read that suggested positive ways to build a violence-free community. As efforts in PNG focus on appointing more women as village magistrates, the committee is attempting to educate the magistrates on how to deal with domestic violence. Thanks to its efforts, police personnel now receive compulsory training on how to act with regard to domestic assaults. The committee is realistic enough to know that the police, in spite of their training, will not be at the forefront in tackling domestic violence in rural areas. But it sees such training as an important step towards convincing rural people that wife-beating is indeed wrong.

One of the best educational resources on the subject is a comprehensive and beautifully illustrated manual on "Sexual and domestic violence: Help, recovery and action in Zimbabwe", compiled by Jill Taylor and Sheelagh Stewart in 1991. Research in Zimbabwe had made it obvious that victims must have access to support at the local community level. The manual provides detailed information on the different kinds of support available to the victims of sexual assault and domestic violence, including medical and legal action, and contains a similarly detailed section on counselling victims, including children. Violence against women is defined as a crime, and as a social problem calling for social action including education, training, organizing, and lobbying for change. In a foreword to the manual, Edmund Kahari, the district public relations officer of the Zimbabwe police force, acknowledges that:

> We know that the figure of reported rapes (in 1970, 576 rapes and 17,646 sexual assaults) represents only a fraction of the number of rapes actually committed during the year. The situation regarding wife-beating is equally alarming. We all need to take these problems very seriously. We should try to equip ourselves to help individual victims as well as working to change attitudes towards these crimes.

A similar handbook produced by the Aboriginal and Torres Strait Islander Congress in Australia on "Family violence through black eyes" recognizes that family violence crept into the life of aboriginal communities after colonization. It clearly documents the seriousness of the current situation and analyzes both the causes and possible solutions. The handbook lists possible options for women and abused children, including available legal protection, and proposes a simple workshop to enable communities to deal with the problem of family violence.

Manuals like these are valuable resources in many countries and contexts. Such educational work is rooted in awareness that most societies are uninformed about the different aspects of violence against women and are therefore unable to devise adequate responses. A shocking lack of knowledge of legal provisions is apparent even in "enlightened" societies where women in particular often do not realize that they *can* seek legal redress. In countries with high levels of illiteracy among women, much energy has been devoted to developing simple educational materials to demystify, decode and provide easy access to legal provisions and procedures.

Engagement in educational work has also led women to discover that even where laws for redress do exist, they are ridden with loopholes. It has encouraged them to

challenge not only tardiness in implementation but also
the flaws that make such laws ineffective to curb violence.
The way forms of violence are defined is often ambiguous, as is the definition of consent. More seriously, the
will to punish those guilty of violence against women is
often lacking. Such crimes, however violent and dangerous, are frequently viewed and condoned as "domestic
disputes that should be resolved amicably". Even more
serious is the fact that a woman's past history is still, in
this day and age, drawn into the debate.

Over the past twenty years, women in many countries
have been campaigning for changes in existing laws or for
new ones, and rape and family laws and criminal procedure codes have been revamped as a result. But women
are aware that this is not enough. Patriarchal attitudes run
deep, and the necessary attitudinal changes have not yet
occurred.

Devising new ways to deal with violence

Some novel methods of dealing with violence have
emerged over the past few decades. In Manitoba, Canada,
native American people are using a *circle of healing* to
address violence in their communities. Five or six women
who began meeting secretly to share their own problems
soon realized that they had to extend their work to other
women who were also in need of healing. The group
connected the psychological, emotional and physical violence directed against them to the economic, social and
political underdevelopment of their community. They
realized that unless violence against women was dealt
with, their communities could not move forward.

In the circle of healing, the entire community is treated
to exorcize the pervasive illness of violence. The key to
the circle's healing power is a special gathering where the
victim, the abuser, community and family members come
together to face the situation and the abuser must publicly
acknowledge his crime. Members of the community tell

the abuser how they feel about what has happened, and offer their support for healing. They also talk to the victim and the families involved. The abuser is given a "healing contract" setting out the punishment — usually community work — and arrangements are made to protect the victim. When the contract expires, a cleansing ceremony takes place to symbolize the return of balance to the abuser, the family and the community. At this point, the healing is complete and the crime can be forgotten. Such healing can take years.

Since the 1970s, women have asserted their right to safety on the streets at any time of day or night. Every year in late September at *Take back the night* marches around the world, but mainly in the West, women name the violence that is the source of their fears, thus refusing the enforced silence long used to cloak the reality. The marches are another attempt to create space for women to speak the truth. Their message is their determination to fight back. This includes demanding safety measures, organizing women's self-defence, lobbying for adequate funding for services to women victims, and public education on the issues involved. Although the marches started from the demand to be able to walk on the streets alone at night, the whole spectrum of violence against women has been highlighted in recent years and the links between racism, homophobia and violence against women exposed.

The Philippines-based Asian Women's Human Rights Commission has *widened the scope of human rights* by insisting that all forms of violence against women — sex tourism, dowry deaths and other forms of domestic violence, pornography, rape, sex-specific forms of torture — are violations of human rights. Among their public awareness-raising strategies are fact-finding missions to trouble areas, international public hearings on Asian women's human rights cases, tribunals on women's issues, and a "declaration on human rights of women of the South". The commission has supported the struggle of Korean "comfort women" (forced to "service" Japanese soldiers during World War II) to obtain adequate compensation.

When Peruvian women in some Lima neighbourhoods *demonstrated directly in front of houses* where domestic violence was known to have occurred, the incidence of wife-abuse dropped slightly. This technique has been used by women in many contexts in the South, particularly in remote villages where they know that they have only each other to rely on for protection.

In India too, when it was becoming clear that neither the police nor the law courts would protect women who were murdered for dowry (the cases often being registered as suicides), women likewise took matters into their own hands by demonstrating in front of homes where dowry murders had taken place, in order to shame the family into acknowledging its guilt. As well as making clear their determination to deal with individual perpetrators of violence, women have also found ways of protecting their sisters against violence before it happens. In some Indian villages, each woman is given a whistle. The moment she blows it is a signal to other women that she is threatened and needs their support. Then they run to her rescue, threatening the abuser until he stops.

Outdoor theatre dramatizing the different forms that violence against women can take is the methodology used by the "Groundwork Theatre Action Company" and "Teens in Action" in Kingston, Jamaica. In one of the situations they portray, a young girl pleads with her father not to "do that" to her while her mother is away. After the show, the actors engage the audience in a consciousness-raising discussion. "Sistren" is another Caribbean theatre troupe that uses drama as a medium of education and awareness-raising on women's issues.

In the United States, women at one university started a campaign to denounce "date rapists" by *writing their names on bathroom walls*, and students at another university organized a candlelight vigil to demand greater action on "date rapes".

Over the past two decades, since the need to provide temporary shelter to women whose lives are endangered was recognized, *women's crisis and refuge centres* have opened in many countries. Most battered women do not leave home because they do not know where else to go. Often, they do not want family and friends to know what they are going through, and sometimes they know that the home of a family member or friend is not safe either since the abuser can follow them there. Women who have been raped also need safety.

In some crisis and refuge centres, trained lawyers and counsellors offer legal advice and psychological and medical help. The company of other women who have gone through a similar trauma can be highly therapeutic. In such centres, a newcomer may feel she has finally found real understanding and genuine support. By talking with and listening to others, she understands that she is not alone. Slowly, she identifies with others and begins to develop self-esteem, along with the hope that she too can free herself and change her relationships with others.

Women's refuge centres are now being set up in almost every country in the world, sometimes with state support. Often, however, they are managed on shoestring budgets, and are unable to give the full support that all who come to them deserve. Sometimes they must turn women away. The state, the church and the community have not yet realized how important it is for women to sustain each other in this way. Shelters are seen as more institutions whose infrastructure needs to be maintained. The fact that they are usually run on a voluntary basis by women who give their time and energy to provide a haven of support for other women is forgotten. For women whose bodies and souls have been wounded by violence, they may be the only hope.

By daring to identify the various forms of violence they experience and taking steps to end it, women are declaring that they will be passive victims no longer. Over the past two decades, women of all sectors, in urban and rural settings, of all religious persuasions and races, in all nations and regions have been transcending the paralyzing emotions felt by being the victims of forces beyond their control, and are initiating creative action for change. A slogan, "the personal is political", has given them the power to transform their pain into political power in order to usher in a world of greater justice and peace.

Hong Kong feminist theologian Kwok Pui Lan tells the story of two powerful women — Zhang Zhi-xin of China, and Suk Wah of Korea — who suffered greatly at the hands of the state. Describing how they were transformed by their experiences, she commented: "In the struggle of Asian people… many Zhi-xins and Suk Wahs must have heard the cry of the people and felt their pain… They are one with the people and their hearts are touched by their pain. It is this passion that makes them identify with the exploited, that motivates and empowers them to rectify wrong, to fight for justice."[21]

Sharadamma comes from a lower middle-class background and lost her daughter on the altar of greed for more dowry. For a long time, she could not believe what had happened, or that she would never see justice done because the police had been bribed and the case registered as a suicide. Sharadamma, a simple Indian woman struggling to keep her family going, was suddenly confronted with grave injustice. She describes this as a conversion experience: since then she has devoted her life to work with women and the families of women murdered in family violence. Here are three verses from an epitaph from a mother to her murdered daughter that Sharadamma inspired me to compose:

O daughter of mine,
I loved you.

When you said you would not go back,
Pleaded with me, cried endless tears,
Showed me the scars of the wounds he had inflicted on you,
I knew you would die.
But I closed my eyes, my ears, my heart to your entreaties.
Believe me,
I loved you.

O daughter of mine,
I love you.
You lie there a heap of lifeless ashes.
I feel the pain you bore as the flames devoured you.
I hear with terror your shrill cries of pain.
Forgive me my now-useless tears,
My lack of courage, my silence when I should have spoken.
Believe me,
I love you.

O daughter of mine,
I love you,
For a woman you have made of me.
No longer will I remain entombed in silence.
No longer will my daughter or any other daughter burn.
I thank you for teaching me the power of womanhood.
Believe me,
I love you, I love you, I love you... [22]

It is in this sense that the women's movement of the past 20 years represents "not merely an oppositional force fuelled by anger, a rather negative reaction to oppression, but the development of a distinctive female culture, a positive creative force inspiring men and women alike". [23]

This shift has encouraged concerned and sensitive men in all parts of the world to confront their own sexuality and abuse of power, and to support women in their struggles. Michael Kaufman, an educator on male violence, describes men's dilemma in this way:

At the individual level, the best way to show yourself and the world that you have power and control is by exercising it around you, over those human beings who are defined as not having any, that is, women and children. Violence becomes a terrific means for a man to say to himself that he is a man because he can dominate someone who clearly is not.

The violence and power of individual men is based on their social power, but also on their very real terror, real isolation, real alienation and real fear, which recreate the need for them to control others. The social power of men creates the possibility to act on that need. [24]

Just as women have for centuries denied themselves freedom by seeking refuge in internalized self-abnegation, so men have sought refuge in institutions and structures of domination, not least of all military power, in order to avoid having to face up to their fears.

Michael Kaufman is hopeful that real change is possible. Men can use their influence to ensure that stricter penalties against violence are applied. They can promote peaceful solutions to conflict in every sphere of life, including international relations. Men can develop skills of relating, caring and bonding based on love and commitment to the other.

Small groups of men in solidarity with women, seeking their own liberation as they give moral support to women who are discovering theirs, have sprung up in many parts of the world. These groups are signs of hope whose importance should not be underestimated. Women cannot be held responsible for "educating" men into new patterns of respect and relationship. It is up to the men.

Other signs of hope

It is important to recognize that some governments are taking positive action, reviewing existing laws to ensure that victims have access to legal redress. Of course, the struggle for full and comprehensive legal protection must continue as long as the pain women experience continues to be trivialized in police stations and law courts. But there has been considerable progress in many countries thanks to women's valiant efforts to ensure justice.

The UN Commission on the Status of Women at its March 1991 meeting in Vienna continued to press for further action on this issue. A Canadian resolution recommended the creation of an international instrument to address the issue of violence against women in all its forms, and called upon the UN Division for the Advancement of Women (DAW) to convene a meeting of experts to that end.

The call was repeated at a meeting convened by the Organization of American States in Caracas, Venezuela, in August 1991. Considering the viability of an inter-American convention on women and violence, the meeting agreed that:

> It would be highly advisable to undertake the development of an international instrument to deal with the general typification of gender-specific manifestations of violence, the obligation of states in this area, a definition of minimal rights and remedies to be afforded and the mechanisms to ensure the foregoing. The participants agreed that the suggested convention should address the issues of prevention, punishment and eradication of violence against women in its different manifestations. [25]

On the recommendation of its Commission on the Status of Women, the UN Economic and Social Council (ECOSOC) on 30 May 1991 (in resolution 1991/18) urged member states to adopt, strengthen and enforce legislation prohibiting violence against women, and to take appropriate administrative, social and educational measures to protect women from all forms of physical and mental violence.

High-level representatives of governments, non-governmental organizations and the UN system in five Andean countries (Bolivia, Colombia, Ecuador, Peru and Venezuela) participating in a strategic planning conference organized in Quito in October 1991 by the UN Development Fund for Women, declared that preventing violence against women is a development priority. The declaration recognizes that "violence against women is a universally acknowledged problem" as well as being "one of the most serious obstacles to the enhancement of the living conditions and participation of women" in Latin America and the Caribbean. "Acts of violence against women are a clear violation of basic human rights," the declaration noted.

Ministers from 16 western European nations meeting in Brussels in March 1991 issued a set of 30 specific recommendations to their governments in which they committed themselves "to stimulate all members of concerned governments to pay particular attention to problems related to physical and sexual violence against women". Future meetings are to deal with issues such as violence against children and young girls, prostitution, pornography, the sex trade, physical and sexual violence among minority groups, and sexual harassment in the workplace.

In 1991, the European Community Commission proposed the adoption of a code of conduct prohibiting sexual harassment in the workplace throughout the Community. The proposal is a non-binding recommendation to governments rather than a directive requiring legislation in all 12 countries. The code broadly defines sexual harassment as "unwanted conduct of a sexual nature or other conduct affecting the dignity of women and men at work". It advises employers, unions and employees on practical prevention measures, including publication of workplace standards that expressly forbid sexual harassment, diligent internal investigation of complaints, and formal disciplinary procedures. Research in several EC member-states showed that certain groups, including divorced women, homosexuals, new employees, minorities, and women assigned to non-traditional tasks, are particularly vulnerable to harassment.[26]

Both governmental and nongovernmental organizations in the Caribbean have begun to address the question of violence against women by opening crisis centres, shelters, support networks, and legal aid clinics. State desks whose primary purpose is to assist the victims of sexual abuse are another sign that governments in the region are beginning to take this problem seriously; several states have amended their laws while model legislation on sexual offences is being considered by CARICOM governments.

Of course, there is a wide gap between governments' and international organizations' stated goals and plans and what happens in women's daily lives. Statistics in fact show that in spite of all government claims, violence against women is on the increase, and the state in many instances has been party to the violation of women's basic survival rights.

Violence against women: a human rights issue

For the past two years, women around the world have been organizing "Sixteen days of activism against gender violence". Beginning on November 25 (the International Day Against Violence Against Women declared by Latin American and Caribbean feminists to commemorate the brutal murder of two sisters in the Dominican Republic in 1960), and ending on December 10 (the anniversary of the 1948 Universal Declaration of Human Rights), the "Sixteen days" includes World AIDS Day (December 1) and the anniversary of the Montreal massacre of fourteen women college students (December 6). The campaign seeks to highlight the universal existence of gender violence, create awareness that it violates human rights, and empower women to take leadership on this issue.

During the 1991 "Sixteen days", hundreds of women's groups around the world sponsored public demonstrations, panels, meetings with authorities and policy-makers, radio and television programmes, petition drives, special editions of newsletters, and poster campaigns to protest gender violence. A worldwide petition drive calling on the UN World Conference on Human Rights (Vienna, June 1993) to focus on women's human rights collected more than 200,000 signatures. Addressed to the UN secretary-general, the petition urged the Conference (the first of its kind in 25 years) to expand the definition of human rights violations to include gender violence.

In an opening statement to a February 1992 UN workshop on "Global strategies for achieving gender fairness in the courts: Eliminating violence against women", the UN under-secretary-general for human rights, Jan Martensen, affirmed:

> The issue of violence against women is a growing concern of the UN. The Nairobi "Forward-Looking Strategies for the Advancement of Women to the Year 2000" [formulated by the End-UN Women's Decade meeting there in 1985] reflects the international community's recognition that violence against women exists in various forms in everyday life in all societies. Such violence is a major obstacle to the achievement of peace and other objectives of the UN.
>
> ...I [have] underlined the importance of a holistic approach to human rights... [since] decisions in many areas of activity have an impact on respect for the human rights of women and, in turn, respect for women's rights will positively affect the rights of others. It has become evident that the promotion of enjoyment of human rights of women must be an integral part of our whole approach of promoting human rights. [27]

Whether the commitment with which Mr Martensen credits the UN will be reflected in its work remains to be seen. Amnesty International has been more specific about what needs to be urgently done. Its "Twelve steps to protect women's human rights" include the prevention and punishment of rape, sexual abuse and other ill-treatment by government agents; persecution because of family connections; ill treatment of women refugees, asylum-seekers and women from ethnic minorities; judicial and extrajudicial executions, "disappearances", and the death penalty. Other necessary steps are provision of adequate health care for all detainees and prisoners; immediate and unconditional release of all prisoners of conscience; prompt and fair trials for all political prisoners; protection of women's human rights in situations of armed conflict; ratification of international human rights instruments, and support for the work of relevant intergovernmental organizations.

Amnesty asserts that:

> Governments are responsible yet often fail to take action to prevent human rights abuses. The international community can play a decisive role in protecting human rights through vigilant and concerted action. Important steps towards protecting women's human rights worldwide include documenting human rights violations, publicizing these as widely as possible, and campaigning to press government authorities for an end to the abuses. Governments which fail to protect fundamental human rights should be confronted with the force of international public opinion. [28]

But even Amnesty has failed to view *all* forms of violence against women as human rights violations. In the meantime, violence is a routine experience for women in every nation, causing untold suffering and despair. Behind the statistics are individuals — women whose bodies and souls are deeply wounded by rape, sexual assault, abuse and battery, each a victim of forces beyond her control.

3. Whither the Church?

The World Council of Churches strives to bring together a community of solidarity and mutual concern where faith and principles are expressed in appropriate action. Such a community will not accept violence against women, which is an intolerable manifestation of unequal power relations between women and men. When human sin breaks the trust in this community, Christians are called to assist, to be Christ present for those who struggle for their dignity and rights, to manifest concern for the welfare of others and loving kindness to people in need. A fundamental respect for each human being includes a commitment to the rights and dignity of women. [29]

There are many stories of broken trust within the Christian community. A few years ago, we heard of a woman whose pastor husband made a habit of beating her and then going out with other women. On a friend's advice, she complained to the bishop of her church. He suggested that she call on him if it happened again. Yet when she did phone him, late at night, the bishop asked: "How do I know you are telling the truth?"

At one theological college in India, young men being trained for ministry claimed their "cultural right" to beat their wives! There was also the case of the Indian lay preacher who left his young wife and child to go to Africa to do "the Lord's work". A few months later, he wrote expressing deep concern because he would have to desert her. God had spoken to him and asked him to marry a woman who worked with him...

Church statements condemning violence against women are still few and far between, or are incorporated into other statements so that the specificity of women's experiences of abuse does not get the attention it deserves. Furthermore, although some voices have been raised against clergy misconduct and domestic violence over the past ten years and some churches have acted on the issue, much remains unsaid and the churches have been slow to express their concern.

Sexual harassment and abuse in church contexts or at ecumenical gatherings is a fact to be recognized and roundly condemned. It is imperative that every Christian denomination discuss it and prepare adequate theological and pastoral responses.

Strong pressure from women in its member churches to do something concrete on the issue led the World Council of Churches (WCC) in 1991 to appoint a task-force on violence against women. Composed of five men and five women, it meets regularly and has produced a pastoral/educational brochure (quoted at the beginning of this chapter) which is now available in the Council's four official languages, and is distributed to all participants at WCC-organized meetings and conferences. In the pipeline is a series of seminars to prepare WCC staff to deal with possible cases of sexual harassment at such meetings. A clause stating that "sexual harassment and all forms of related violence will not be tolerated or condoned and offenders will be held responsible for their behaviour, and will be subject to appropriate disciplinary action" was incorporated in the WCC staff rules and regulations in 1993.[30]

In spite of some attempts to challenge the churches to action, domestic violence or clergy sexual misconduct with trusting parishioners are still taboo subjects in many nations in the South. The churches in these countries too have, by and large, maintained silence on the issue. Musimbi Kanyoro, executive secretary for women in church and society with the Lutheran World Federation, reports that:

> Even though women in North America and to a lesser extent in Europe are beginning to speak out about sexual harassment, there is still much reluctance in many societies in the world to discuss issues of sexual violence openly. Many women who have been victims of violence feel guilty because they have been socialized to believe that they provoke men's violence towards them.[31]

In many nations of the South, women see a clergyman as akin to God. When their basic trust in a pastor and, through him, in the church, is broken, most women are too afraid and shocked to accuse the perpetrator of the violence. That sexual harassment and abuse by clergy and pastoral counsellors exists in all regions of the world, and that the churches will have to deal with it, must be acknowledged. Kanyoro emphasizes that:

> It is only in the recent past that churches have begun discussions on this topic. The rude discovery that even church ministers are violent to women challenges the church to overcome the temptation to be trapped in its own culture. The righteousness of the church must include social responsibility as well as individual morality... If the church does not speak out against violence inflicted on women, then by its silence and non-action it is compromising its prophetic call. [32]

Some churches *have* responded. The following sampling of policy positions, training and workshop manuals and guidelines for redress all indicate that there is hope that the church will and can tackle this problem.

The *Canadian Conference of Catholic Bishops* in a 1991 statement entitled "To live without fear", declared that "violence against women breaks the fifth commandment. It is a sin, a crime and a serious social problem... Helpful, compassionate and just responses to women who are victims of violence are important and needed. Long-term strategies for prevention are critical."

The *Anglican Church of Canada* has an excellent report, prepared by its taskforce on violence against women and presented to its general synod in 1986, that focuses on wife abuse. The report holds that "many Christians remain unaware of the extent to which the church has been implicated in condoning and even supporting the behaviour of husbands when they physically punished their wives. Indeed, the church defined such 'discipline' as the bounden duty of a husband in order to correct his wife's soul. A second reason Christians should take pains to confront this particular form of abuse is that theological legitimization has served to reinforce other cultural rationalizations, such as 'a man's home is his castle', so that wife-battering has been trivialized and rendered invisible."

A *United Church of Canada (UCC)* statement against sexual harassment in the church provides clear guidelines for action by employers and institutions to deal with victims and victimizers. A UCC educational brochure entitled "Women in abusive relationships: The church has been silent for too long" lists some of the causes, and suggests that "religion alone is not responsible for such a catalogue of evils, but it contributes to them and even blesses them at times. Change comes slowly and the churches have not been leaders in bringing it about. Our concerns have been the sanctity of the family, reconciliation, restoring marriages, when often the first need is for an end to violence, for safety for women and children and for justice for the oppressed." The brochure indicates what abused women need and what each person or congregation can do in response.

The general assembly of the *Presbyterian Church (USA)* has adopted its own policy and procedures on sexual misconduct. A policy statement makes clear that "sexual misconduct is a violation of ministerial, employment and professional relationships and is never permissible." A theological statement on the issue has also been approved. These instruments are intended to "prevent any person from obtaining and maintaining an unwarranted position of power".

The findings of a 1988 study on sexual harassment in the church by the *United Methodist Church* in the USA in which 1578 clergy and lay people, including church workers, college and seminary students participated, revealed the extent of the problem and led to the conclusion that the issue needs urgent attention. A UMC Board of Global Ministries service centre educational packet on ministries with women in crisis suggests possible responses to such violence against women as physical violence, rape, domestic abuse; sexual exploitation (including sexual harassment), prostitution, pornography; economic exploitation; widowhood, divorce, drug and alcohol abuse, depression and imprisonment.

In the Netherlands, the *Reformed Churches in the Netherlands* and the *Netherlands Reformed Church* have agreed that women who experience sexual abuse or harassment within church structures need more help. Pastors across the country are to be specially trained to receive such complaints and carry out confidential investigations, and a preparatory course on "the pastor's role and intimate questions" was held in the fall of 1991.[33]

The *Uniting Church in Australia* with representatives from the *Uniting Aboriginal and Islander Christian Congress* commission on women and men have produced a brochure on sexual violence in the church community entitled "Break the silence... and the truth shall set you free".

The Latin American Council of Churches department of women's and children's ministries has produced illustrated booklets on violence against women and children as part of an effort to educate congregations on the extent of the problem, and provide guidelines on what Christian communities can do to support victims.

At the VIth assembly of the *All Africa Conference of Churches* in Harare, Zimbabwe, in October 1992, a young woman theologian from Kenya delivered a powerful and very moving sermon on what the kingdom of God means in the context of violence, thereby creating one of the rare occasions when the attention of a major church gathering has focused on this topic!

"Violence is promoted by greed for power and money, desire to dominate and control others," Nyambura

Njoroge said. "It is easy to identify with the violence committed during civil wars and against nature... But I want us to challenge ourselves on the violence and wars that begin right in our bedrooms... the domestic violence that is experienced by women and children in our homes." Njoroge also described unscientific abortion practices, particularly in the context of teenage pregnancies, as "violence against God's creation", and rape as "another violence which is not taken seriously".

The family: a safe place for women and children?

The question of whether the family is a safe place for women and children has to be asked and answered, particularly by the church which has placed so much emphasis on the sacrament of marriage and on family life.

Women have always been the backbone of family life and have held families together in the midst of tensions and changes. And yet, when a woman wishes to opt out of an abusive relationship, she is blamed for breaking the family unit! Confronted with cases of women and children exposed to danger in their homes, fear of violating the sacrament of marriage and the ideal of Christian family life has often paralyzed the churches into inactivity. Both church and community have turned a blind eye to the reality of such situations on the pretext that no one has the right to interfere in a couple's private life.

The subtle message conveyed is that family life is a woman's responsibility and that nothing justifies family breakup. A Canadian woman testifies:

> I was active in the church throughout the 20 years of my marriage, during which I lived in constant fear. I was told by the church that, as a Christian, I was responsible for my children, my husband, my marriage. In fact, whatever happened in the home was my responsibility... The church was my lifeline... It was the only place my husband allowed me to go... But these messages helped me stay in that relationship of fear for a long time.[34]

This testimony reminded me of an Indian woman who suffered daily battering by her husband for nine years. Describing her marriage, this woman explained:

> He was a leader in the church community, serving on the pastorate committee and diocesan council. No one would believe me when I said that this "gentleman" was nearly killing me. We went to church regularly and he would watch me all the time — whom I spoke to and what I did. He remained in the pastorate committee even after I escaped from him, and the bishop has been urging me to reconcile with this man of whom I am so afraid.

Christian women's initiatives

Knowing that it is often difficult to come out of an abusive relationship, women have responded with commitment and compassion to their sisters' suffering.

The Women's Inter-Church Council of Canada has designed a very useful workshop as a resource for theological education. Called "Hands to end violence against women", it uses case studies of women who have experienced violence, examines myths and realities around the issue, analyzes the factors that encourage violence, and suggests action strategies for a community approach to this pervasive evil.

One of the best known and most effective campaigners in this field, who has done extensive work on sexual abuse in the church, Marie M. Fortune directs a centre in Seattle for the prevention of sexual and domestic violence, and many women and denominations in the US and Canada have sought her guidance on how to deal with the issue of sexual misconduct by clergy. The centre received its first call from a victim of sexual abuse by a clergyman in 1983; since then, it has dealt with over 500 cases (averaging three calls a week) from every denomination, and has trained over 2000 religious professionals and leaders from the US and Canada to deal with this concern.

Established in 1987 in Australia, CASA House provides a 24-hour crisis care programme with supportive counselling and public advocacy for women victims. In 1989, several churches funded CASA to do a study on women, the church and sexual violence. The study challenged the church to break its silence on this crime, support the victims and educate the clergy. The next phase of "Project Anna" (so named in honour of the woman who recognized Jesus as the long-awaited liberator) was launched in 1990 to provide an educational and consultative service to the churches on the issue.

In response to a request from women on all sides of the war in the former Yugoslavia, the World Council of Churches in 1992 called on people around the world to wear black on one day of the week as a sign of solidarity and commitment to the raped and violated women there, and in all other wars and conflicts around the world. It is a day not only of mourning but of protest, symbolic of people's determination to struggle for a violence-free world.

4. Women's Theological Visions

> Weep no more my sisters.
> God knows that you weep, and
> She weeps with you.

These words of compassion and comfort were spoken by feminist theologian Elizabeth Bettenhausen in response to what speakers at "the Well", the women's space at the sixth assembly of the World Council of Churches in Canada in 1983, had to say about violence against women. After listening to voices from Palestine, South Africa, Nicaragua, India and Canada, Bettenhausen said that although she could not immediately find words of comfort from the Bible, she could at least share the assurance of God's sorrow over women's tears.

Such faith has empowered women theologians all over the world to seek theological meaning for women's suffering, to go beyond expressing pain to attempting to reconstruct some of the basic theological assumptions that have tended to legitimize it.

In a moving Bible study on rape and patriarchy, for example, WCC deputy general secretary Mercy Oduyoye (a Ghanaian theologian) tells the story of Dinah (Gen. 34) in the latter's own words:

> Being an only daughter and always seeking the company of other daughters, it was in search of companions that I stepped out of my mother's tent. My father had bought land to lay claim to space. I stepped out to claim the space God had given us and to seek the friendship and solidarity of the women of our new neighbourhood.
>
> The brute force that pounced on me and carried me away, kicking and screaming, later took flesh and blood in the person of Shechem, said to be a prince. This royal rapist could not have known who I was, let alone my name. I was but clay in his hands as he pounded and squeezed vigorously until I would yield what would please him. I was just a part of silent nature to be worked until I produced or became what would please men. That I screamed and scratched meant nothing. I was female and should expect to be raped...

Not a word from me is recorded anywhere. That for me is the saddest part. Do I have a say in how my life is managed? Am I and the women I went out to seek just chips on a patriarchal bargaining table?[35]

Oduyoye referred at the start of her Bible study to Phyllis Trible's important contributions to feminist theology. In *Texts of Terror*,[36] Trible traces the lives of four biblical women: Hagar (Gen. 21:9-21), Tamar (2 Sam. 13:1-22), an unnamed concubine (Judg. 11:29-40), and the daughter of Jephthah (Judg. 11:29-40). The stories of these four women who are used, abused, discarded or killed by patriarchal power and lust are virtually unknown, and very few sermons have been preached about their lives. The God of justice and compassion does not intervene to save their lives. Worse, their sacrifice seems to be part of the divine plan.

To Trible and women to whom her hermeneutical model makes sense, these texts of terror are not "relics of a primitive and inferior past" but ring with contemporary overtones. For violated women, God may seem to be absent or strangely silent while the andro-centric Bible, the predominantly male images of God, and the mostly male church hierarchy can symbolize an uncaring church that is blind to the deep pain they experience.

Women hear the silence of the church in distorted teachings and practices, in inadequate preparation of partners for marriage, in one-sided interpretations of biblical passages in the marriage service (like citing Eph. 4:21 as permission for a man to "discipline" his wife to obedience and submission). They hear it in the imposition of a self-effacing docile image of Mary, in liturgy that does not include their experience, in a refusal to believe women's accounts of their own or their sisters' suffering at men's hands.

"Christ suffered and died for you on the Cross. Can't you bear some suffering too?" is a question often addressed, in one form or another, to women when they appeal to the church for succour. Perhaps one of the most pernicious aspects of Christian teaching has been this imposed *theology of sacrifice and suffering*.

A sacrificial lifestyle and a commitment to die for the other are indeed Christ-like qualities that women are willing to continue to emulate in order to protect people's lives and livelihood. Women understand Christ's sacrifice and resurrection as signs of full liberation. As Roman Catholic theologian from the Philippines Mary John Mananzan suggests:

> The experience of the resurrection is the experience of the fully liberated Christ, which is in itself liberating… My experience of liberation in Christ's resurrection also inspires me to continue with courage to struggle with the poor and the oppressed, even in the midst of danger and insecurity, because I have come to understand that it is when I try to save my life that I lose it, and it is by being ready to lose it that I gain it. [37]

But women also ask whether the sacrifice demanded of them has a purpose. As one Indian women's group put it:

> Christ died on the Cross because humankind could not bear his disturbing and uncomfortable message of salvation for the world. By his death, he saved the world from its hypocrisy, apathy and selfishness. He was the scapegoat for a wicked and cruel world. Christ gave of himself for a purpose.
>
> The theology of sacrifice that is thrust on women is of no purpose… Women are the scapegoats of this theology. What they have to discover for themselves is the resurrection element in their sacrifice, as a step towards the discovery of their power. [38]

Arms outstretched as if crucified, the sculpture of the woman by artist Almuth Lutkenhaus-Lackey presently stands on the grounds of Emmanuel College at the University of Toronto. For the women of all faiths and no faith at all who gathered around it in December 1989 to mourn the deaths of 14 brutally murdered Canadian women students, the sculpture expressed the mingling of compassion and suffering of Christ's death.

The 1986 Anglican Church of Canada's taskforce on violence against women report mentioned earlier (see page 42) delves deeper into the concepts of suffering and sacrifice. "Jesus' voluntary suffering and death on the cross cannot and must not be paralleled with the involuntary suffering of women, children or other victims of violence, nor be used to justify their situation in any way."

For Mercy Oduyoye, sacrifice is that which is "freely and consciously made" and is "noble and lovely, loving and motivated by love and gratitude". Violence against women is none of these. "The Christ for me," she says, "is the Jesus of Nazareth who agreed to be God's 'sacrificial lamb', thus teaching that true and living sacrifice is *that which is freely and consciously made...* who approved of the costly sacrifice of the woman with the expensive oil who anointed him in preparation of his burial, thereby also approving all that is noble and lovely, loving and motivated by love and gratitude."[39]

US Methodist ministers Joanne Carlson-Brown and Rebecca Parker take a more radical approach in their ground-breaking article "For God so loved the world":

> Christianity is an abusive theology that glorifies suffering. Is it any wonder that there is so much abuse in modern culture when the predominant image or theology of the culture is of "divine child abuse" — God the Father demanding and carrying out the suffering and death of his own son? If Christianity is to be liberating for the oppressed, it must itself be liberated from this theology.[40]

Black womanist theologian Delores S. Williams takes a similar position:

> My exploration of black women's sources has revealed a heretofore undetected structure of domination... operative in African-American women's lives since slavery. The structure... is surrogacy, and it gives black women's oppression

its unique character, and raises challenging questions about the way redemption is imaged in a Christian context.

God's gift to humans, through Jesus, was to invite them to participate in this ministerial vision ("whosoever will, let them come") of righting relations. The response to this invitation by human principalities and powers was the horrible deed that this cross represents — the evil of humankind trying to kill the ministerial vision of life... Thus, to respond meaningfully to black women's historic experience of surrogacy-oppression, the theologian must show that redemption of humans can have nothing to do with any kind of surrogate role Jesus was reputed to have played in the bloody act that supposedly gained victory over sin/or evil. [41]

For women in violent contexts who have clung to the image of a loving compassionate God and of God's son who so loved the world that he was willing to die for it, such a theological position is difficult to accept. But living in what feminist theologian Mary Hunt calls "a world of contextual violence and episodic justice", we may need to try to understand what it is that these theologians are inviting us to discover. And this may involve looking at violence and the Christian tradition in a more radical way.

Hunt in fact suggests that "those texts, doctrines and practices that perpetuate what today is considered violence, regardless of their historical centrality in the tradition, be dropped". She is aware that she is calling for fundamental change in Christianity when she suggests that "we begin with the basics like the violent death of Jesus, and look fearlessly for alternative ways of articulating meaning and value. Only by doing so," Hunt concludes, "will we be able to say that there is no cause and effect between Christianity and a violent culture, and perhaps in the process we will undo some of the violence. [42]

Clearly, this is a call for a shift from the traditional third-world liberation theology view of the cross. Yet the feeling of oneness with the suffering of Christ has sustained victims of discrimination and oppression for centuries. It assures women that Christ understands if no one else will. Hong Kong feminist theologian Kwok Pui Lan describes the vital significance to Asian women of Christ's suffering:

> It is the person on the cross who suffers like us, was rendered a nobody, who illuminates our tragic existence and speaks to countless women in Asia. We are not looking to Jesus as a mere example to follow, neither shall we try to idolize him. We see Jesus as the God who takes human form and suffers and weeps with us.[43]

Argentinian theologian Nelida Ritchie makes the same point in describing the courage of the "Mothers of the Plaza de Mayo", and a mother's grief when she knows her son has been killed:

> God stands still before such human agony and is moved. Each time the Gospel speaks of human suffering, it shows his (Jesus') complete identification with the other's situation; it shows his creative and active solidarity. Jesus' feelings precipitate changes, a search for the causes, that transform the pain-causing situation.
>
> This ability to "feel with others" leads Jesus to stop hunger, eradicate illness, and remove the burdens that hamper life. His compassion does not stop with saying "Don't cry", but goes on to restore what the person has lost so that tears are replaced by true joy... Resurrection, the giving back of life, like a miracle, is a sign that anticipates the complete transformation for which Christ is responsible. All of us who proclaim the Lordship of Jesus Christ... are called to be in solidarity with those who cry and search, to help restore what is lost to those who mourn.[44]

The final document of the Ecumenical Association of Third-World Theologians intercontinental women's conference (held in Oaxtapec, Mexico, in December 1986) differentiates the suffering that goes with ushering in new life from that which is inflicted by the oppressor and is passively accepted:

Many Christians in our continents are seeking to see in Jesus' suffering, passion, death and resurrection a meaning for their own suffering... Nevertheless, we have a mission to announce that Christ brought new life to humanity and that this was the whole point of his suffering. Suffering that is inflicted by the oppressor and is passively accepted does not lead to life; it is destructive and demonic. But suffering that is part of the struggle for the sake of God's reign or that results from the uncontrollable and mysterious conditions of humankind is rooted in the paschal mystery, evocative of the rhythm of pregnancy, delivery and birth. This kind of suffering is familiar to women at all times, who participate in the pains of birth and the joys of the new creation. [45]

While this is a debate that needs to be pursued, it is clear that senseless suffering can never be legitimized by the cruel death that Christ suffered on the cross. Marie Fortune reminds us that "rather than the sanctification of suffering, Jesus' crucifixion remains a witness to the horror of violence. It is not a model of how suffering should be borne, but a witness of God's desire that no one should have to suffer such violence again." [46]

Another area of Christian teaching that needs to be explored further is that of *forgiving and forgetting*. Women are told that Christ forgave his enemies even as he hung on the cross, beaten and abused by insolent might. But again, the parallel is far from convincing if we think of who violated women are asked to forgive and why.

Some images come to mind. There is the image of the Dutch "comfort woman" forced to "service" Japanese soldiers during World War II who told us that she "had the right not to forgive after 50 years". Or the image of a bruised five-year-old in a slum in Madras who had been raped. Or that of a three-year-old who was sexually abused in a day-care centre by people she and her parents trusted. And there is the image of the woman, mentioned earlier, who had been battered every single day for nine years by her husband, who had lost hearing in one ear, whose arms, legs and breasts bore the tell-tale marks of ruthless violence.

I could not agree more with Mary Hunt when she writes[47] that "such forgiving and forgetting is pathological advice in a culture of violence". The world must understand women's inability to forgive or forget wounds inflicted without meaning on their bodies and souls when no adequate retribution has been made. The glib demand for forgiveness is an injustice, and the traditional emphasis on forgiving and forgetting contributes to an abused woman's oppression. She gives the abuser many chances, covering up for him and pretending that the nightmare is over, hoping that forgiveness will heal the relationship. She is often proved wrong, and sometimes it is too late.

Marie Fortune outlines an ethical framework for dealing with violence against women. Assuming that the basic premise is Micah's admonition to "do justice, love mercy and walk humbly before God" (6:8), she concludes that justice is central to the scriptures and to the church in an attempt to right relationships that are distorted by violence. On that basis:

> Truth-telling, acknowledgment of the violation, compassion, protection of the vulnerable, accountability, restitution and vindication are the requirements for doing justice and mercy in the face of violation and injustice.[48]

Compassion, accountability, restitution and vindication are the norms. Forgiveness comes later, Hunt says:

> Forgiveness is possible in the aftermath of physical abuse only if the person who has been subjected to it has been assured of personal safety, and is no longer subjected to verbal or psychological abuse. Even after all abuse has ceased, forgiveness is a long process. A person recovering from abuse should not be burdened with the unrealistic expectations of a pastoral worker who wants the person to "forgive and forget". Not only the abused person's rights but

their very being has been violated, and they need an oppor-
tunity to vent their anger and rage.

Forgiving oneself can be the hardest task for a victim
whose self-image has been shattered... Real forgiveness
comes at the final stage of a long process through which
victims regain control of their lives. [49]

Marie Fortune holds that forgiveness becomes an
option *if* some form of justice is done. The word "vindication" best describes what needs to happen before a victim
is able to forgive. As Fortune points out:

Ultimately, vindication for the victims is the substance of
justice and mercy. Vindication refers not to vengeance and
retaliation but to the exoneration and justification of those
who have experienced harm, made legitimate complaints,
and consequently been imputed. Surely the physical, emotional and spiritual key to healing from violation is to be set
free from the multiple layers of suffering it created. [50]

Many women would assert that the *hierarchical dualism* of Christian theology and ecclesiology has been at the
root of much violence against women. A tradition which
is built on a hierarchy of power relations — God above
humanity, the priest above the congregation, and men
above women — seems to be sanctioning the abuse of
power and makes women in congregations among the
most vulnerable and susceptible to that abuse. To deal
adequately with this issue calls for a new look at ecclesiology as it has been understood and practised. But is the
church ready for this?

The statement by the Presbyterian Church in the USA
cited earlier (see page 43) acknowledges this problem and
suggests the need for an alternative way of dealing with it:

A problem that occurs in traditional procedures for
redressing grievances when it comes to sexual harassment is
that the abuser is most often higher in the hierarchical
structure of the organization than is the abused. This problem also occurs within the structure of the church. As a

result, there needs to be an alternate route within our judicatory system for dealing with sexual harassment.

But will an "alternate route" suffice? Is it not time for the church to discover how power has been systematically abused to dominate the powerless? Should not the church clearly state that the hierarchical patterns of leadership and ministry which have perpetuated this abuse of power, keeping women and children in a state of fear and insecurity, are sinful? Is the church ready for this?

The church's *reluctance to deal with the issue of human sexuality* also has a bearing on the violence in our societies. This question must also be addressed if we are to be able to fully understand the roots of the violence. All religious traditions have tended to convey warped images of sexuality, providing quasi-divine legitimization for rape and abuse of women's bodies. It is therefore easier to discuss, for example, the economic and political roots of prostitution than the reasons why men seek out prostitutes. The church would rather take a moralistic stand on the women involved than challenge the men to examine their depraved sexuality. The church is quick to oppose abortion even in wartime rather than look compassionately at the future of broken women and of children born out of brutal lust. Pope John Paul II, for example, urged the raped women of Bosnia-Herzegovina to bear their violators' children rather than choose abortion. In a letter to the archbishop of Sarajevo, he wrote that "even in such a tragic situation, [these women] must be helped to distinguish between the act of deplorable violence which they have suffered from men who have lost all reason and conscience, and the reality of these new human beings who have been given life."

It is ironical that women have been simultaneously viewed as child-bearers and evil temptresses. Warped images of sexuality hold women responsible for the advent of evil in the world. The Indian epic *Ramayana* includes a story about the sage Vishwamitra, who is absorbed in penance so intense that it shakes the whole universe, including the heavens and the throne of the lord of lords, Indra himself. Annoyed, Indra sends the beautiful Menaka to earth to dance her way into the soul of the devout sage. Menaka ultimately touches the sage seductively and wakes him out of his trance, enticing him to take her into his arms. The penance is broken, the heavens stop shaking, and Indra recovers his peace.

In Christianity, women have been identified as the source of impurity and death, and their victimization legitimized by attributing the origin of evil and sin to Eve. Through Eve, "man" is said to have lost his immortality, and woman her essential freedom, the evil in the world being epitomized by the pain of childbirth. The dualism in Christianity between male/female, spirit/body, human/non-human and good/evil helps to validate the low status accorded to women. And since "evil" is associated with female, it is a woman's fault if she is raped. It is she who enticed the man to rape her; as popular parlance has it, she "asked for it".

In working with battered women in Minnesota, USA, Joy Bussert reflected on how this aspect of Christian theology has influenced the women's lives:

> Christian theologians like Luther projected "uncontrollable sensuality", and thus responsibility for the fall, onto women as the object of sexuality since sexuality appears to be what they most feared in themselves. Thus [did the theologians] make woman the unfortunate recipient of the Christian adaptation of Platonic alienation (of the soul) from the body, and relegated her to her "rightful" — that is, subordinate — place in relation to man. The higher principles, mind and spirit, were labelled "male" and the lower principles, body and matter, were labelled female. Man represented mind, woman represented body. Man had the capacity for reason and intellect, woman the capacity for emotion and feeling. Man became the rational subject; woman the carnal object. [51]

These theologians fail to consider that in Christ all these odious distinctions were overcome. He tore down the body-soul dualism by accepting women as they were, including their bodies. Some of the moving encounters Jesus had with women spring immediately to mind. We think, for instance, of the unconditional love expressed by the unnamed woman who washed Jesus' feet with oil and wiped them with her hair, or of the faith of the haemorrhaging woman who defied all accepted norms of pollution by touching the hem of his robe, and who received not only healing but acceptance and commendation for her faith.

5. Where Do We Go from Here?

> Christians are called to assist, to be Christ present for those who struggle for their dignity and rights[52]

Is the church present in the pain and suffering of the millions of violated women in this world? The church has been in the vanguard in challenging global economic and political injustice, and articulate in condemning policies and practices that keep millions of people subjugated. As has been rightly said, movements of oppressed peoples for justice and dignity are a spiritual necessity of our times. Then why is the church not a fore-runner in challenging all the forces that hold women ransom to a violent and ruthless world? Why has the theology of the church been virtually silent on this issue? Why has the church in many instances condoned sexual harassment and even violence in its own institutional life? These are the questions women are asking as we call on the church to respond with resolute action.

Solidarity means "being ready to be touched by the other", WCC general secretary Konrad Raiser said recently. What does this mean for the church? Is it ready to immerse itself in the bleeding lives of women, to be touched by our wounded hands? Is the church ready to respond to our vision of a violence-free world, based on our theological and spiritual resources?

Jesus heard women's cries. He not only shared some important insights into the purpose and meaning of his life and ministry with the simple Samaritan woman at the well, but he also acknowledged the context of personal and structural pain in which she was immersed. Jesus gathered the woman's tears and baptized her into a renewed and transformed life. She left her past, symbolized by her water jar, behind her and ran into the town to share with her people the message of salvation she had received.

If we were to gather together the tears already shed and as yet unshed by women around the world, I believe we could baptize the church into a life of solidarity and resolute action.

The women raped in all wars and conflicts, including those who must bear unwanted babies, the women who have been subject to harassment and abuse in pastoral relationships and ecumenical gatherings, the women who have escaped from unsafe homes, the women who have sold their children into prostitution after a life of prostitution themselves — these and many other women call on the church to listen to their cries, but also to support them in their efforts to overcome their pain. They are clear that such solidarity is possible only if the church is ready and willing to support them in their efforts to create a safe space, a secure and free environment, in which they may fearlessly work towards a just and peaceful world for all.

And women say:

Do you wonder that a storm brews
Within a woman who is counted as soft?
Do not be disturbed!
Even now,
Without your solidarity,
We have no intention
Of crossing the storm
Which is our struggle for freedom.
There is a lot of old dirt
Both in your brain and my brain.
Come, let us clean it out and move on.
We should not be fighting each other.
We must be together setting right the wrong in this world.

But before this...
If your legs happen to be on my hands,
Just move them a little bit.

Subhadra
(Translated from the original Tamil)

Notes

[1] *MATCH News*, Canada, 1990.

[2] The examples that follow are taken from the International Women's Tribune Centre quarterly newsletter *The Tribune*, no. 46, June 1991.

[3] *African Woman*, no. 6, July-October 1992.

[4] Several other studies make the same point; cf. *International Herald Tribune*, 6 November 1991.

[5] Charlotte Bunch, "Women's Rights as Human Rights: Toward a Re-Vision of Human Rights", in *Gender Violence: A Development and Human Rights Issue*, Centre for Women's Global Leadership, Rutgers University, USA, 1991.

[6] These statistics are taken from *The Tribune, op. cit.*

[7] "Patriarchy and Violence Against Women", in *Hands to End Violence Against Women*, Women's Inter-Church Council of Canada, Toronto, 1988.

[8] "Sexual Harassment: A Hidden Issue", Project on the Status and Education of Women, USA.

[9] Véronique Ducret, "Harcèlement sexuel sur les lieux de travail", in *Questions au féminin*, February 1992.

[10] Quoted in *Korea Times*, 2 December 1992.

[11] *Madhu Bhushan*, Vimochana, a feminist group in Bangalore, India.

[12] Quoted in *In God's Image*, vol. 10, no. 2, summer 1991.

[13] *African Woman, op. cit.*; the account of the rape is from *Time*, 12 August 1991.

[14] "Rape and Sexual Abuse: Torture and Ill-Treatment of Women in Detention", in *ACT* no. 77, Amnesty International, November 1991.

[15] Catrin Davies in "Free and Equal in Dignity and Rights? The Trafficking of Women to Europe", Quaker Council of European Affairs, Brussels, August 1992.

[16] *Women's World*, no. 24, quoted in "Women Educating to End Violence against Women", Popular Education Research Group, Toronto, Canada, September 1992.

[17] *WARC Update*, World Alliance of Reformed Churches, Geneva, spring 1992.

[18] Foundation for Women, Thailand.

[19] *Exchange and Mart*, 31 October 1991.

[20] The following statistics on Europe are taken from Catrin Davies, *op. cit.*

[21] "God Weeps with Our Pain", in *New Eyes for Reading: Biblical and Theological Reflections from Third World Women*, eds J.S. Pobee and B. Wartenberg-Potter, WCC, Geneva, 1986.

[22] Aruna Gnanadason, poem published in *Indian Express*, no. 3, April 1986.

[23] Rama Joshi and Joanna Riddle, *Daughters of Independence. Gender, Caste and Class in India*, Kali for Women, 1986.

[24] From a conversation between Michael Kaufman and psychotherapist Eimear O'Neill, quoted in *Men's Violence, Women's World*, no. 26, ISIS-WICCE, winter 1991-92.

[25] *CIM Doc.* no. 1, Inter-American Commission of Women, Organization of American States, 1991.

[26] *International Herald Tribune*, 3 July 1991.

[27] From the opening statement by Jan Martensen at a UN Workshop on "Global Strategies for Achieving Gender Fairness in the Courts", Geneva, February 1992.

[28] From "Women in the Frontline" campaign material, Amnesty International, 1990.

[29] "When Christian Solidarity Is Broken", WCC, Geneva, 1992.

[30] *Staff Rules and Regulations*, chap. VI, World Council of Churches.

[31] Musimbi Kanyoro, from the first in a series of lectures at Augustana University College, Alberta, Canada, March 1992.

[32] *Ibid.*

[33] *epd ZA*, no. 130, 10 July 1991.

[34] Quoted by Shirley Jane Endicott in "Theology and Violence against Women", *Women's Concerns*, Canada, winter 1991.

[35] Mercy Oduyoye, Bible study presented at a preparatory meeting for the July 1993 Ecumenical Global Gathering of Youth and Students (EGGYS), Geneva, February 1993.

[36] Fortress Press, Philadelphia, 1984.

[37] Mary John Mananzan, "Who is Jesus Christ?", in *Christologies in Encounter, Voices from the Third World*, vol. XI, no. 2, EATWOT publication, December 1989.

[38] "The National Situation: A Biblical Response from Women", in *Stree Reflect Series*, no. 1, All India Council of Christian Women/ National Council of Churches in India, 1986.

[39] Mercy Oduyoye, "An African Woman's Christ", in *Christologies in Encounter, op. cit.*, emphasis added.

[40] Joanne Carlson Brown and Rebecca Parker, *Christianity, Patriarchy and Abuse: A Feminist Critique*, Pilgrim Press, New York, 1989.

[41] Delores S. Williams, "Black Women's Surrogacy Experience and the Christian Notion of Redemption", in *After Patriarchy: Feminist Transformations in World Religions*, Orbis, Maryknoll, NY, 1992.

[42] Mary Hunt, "Waging War at Home: Christianity and Structural Violence", in *Miriam's Song V*, Priests for Equality, 1992.

[43] Kowk Pui Lan, "God Weeps with Our Pain", *op. cit.*

[44] Nelida Ritchie, "Women and Christology", in *Through Her Eyes: Women's Theology from Latin America*, ed. Elsa Tamez, Orbis, Maryknoll, NY, 1989.

[45] Quoted by Mercy Oduyoye in "Third World Women Doing Theology", *With Passion and Compassion*, ed. Virginia Fabella, Orbis, Maryknoll, NY, 1990.

[46] Marie Fortune, "Family Violence: A Workshop Manual", Centre for the Prevention of Sexual and Domestic Violence, Seattle, USA, 1980.

[47] Mary Hunt in "Waging War...", *op. cit.*

[48] Marie Fortune, *Is Nothing Sacred? When Sex Invades the Pastoral Relationship*, Harper and Row, New York, 1989.

[49] "Ending Violence in Families", United Church of Canada report, 1988.

[50] Marie Fortune, *Is Nothing Sacred?*, *op. cit.*, 1989.

[51] Joy Bussert, *Battered Women: From a Theology of Suffering to an Ethic of Empowerment*, Lutheran Church in America, 1986.

[52] "When Christian Solidarity is Broken", *op. cit.*

Some Resources

This list of books, articles and church statements is far from exhaustive. There is a great deal of material available in many countries of the world. This is only a sampling of the kinds of resources available.

Australia

Australian Council of Churches

"Breaking the Silence: The Church and Domestic Violence", 1986 (a resource package on domestic violence, including a leaders' guide, myths, case studies, a liturgy, theological response).

CASA House (Centre against Sexual Assault)

Note: Most of the resource packages of CASA House contain extensive bibliographies and other helpful material, not all of which are listed here.

"Project Anna", set up to provide advocacy for victims of sexual assault within church communities. (This project, funded by the Uniting Church in Australia, the Roman Catholic Church, the Salvation Army, the Anglican Church, the Baptist Union and the Churches of Christ in Australia, reports one-two such cases per week over the preceding 18 months.)

"A Pastoral Report to Churches on Sexual Violence against Women and Children of the Church Community", Melbourne 1991 (includes Bible stories, prayers, etc.).

Information package (contains brochures on women and rape, including "Rape: Men's Responsibility", and a guide to supporting victims of sexual assault).

Information package on sexual harassment (including a guide for employers: "Sexual Harassment in the Workplace").

Pamphlet "Stopping Sexual Assault in Marriage: A Guide for Women Counselors and Advocates", 1990.

"Give Us Water for the Journey", a liturgy celebrated at "Women Space", WCC Seventh Assembly, Canberra, 1991.

SHIVER (Sexual Harassment Is Violence: we need Effective Redress to stop it)

"Women and Men Working for Change around Sexual Issues in the Church", an organization of the Uniting Church in Australia formed in

1990, publishes a newsletter and works to support and advocate in favour of women bringing complaints of sexual offence against clerics.

Uniting Church: Commission on Women and Men working to develop sexual harassment guidelines (in consultation with CASA House)

Helen Just and Jan Tully, "There Is No Going Back" (relates the experience of two project workers in the Anglican community).

Assembly of the UC Commission on Women and Men, working to develop sexual harassment guidelines, in consultation with CASA House.

"Sexual Violence in the Churches", UCA Commission on Women and Men.

Text of the resolution on sexual violence passed at the Sixth Assembly of the UCA, July 1991.

"Pastoral Report to the Churches on Sexual Violence against Women and Children of the Church Community", proposed for study by the church, July 1991.

"Sexism — What Men Can Do", 1991.

"Thursdays in Black, A-gender", the UC Assembly Commission on Women and Men, March 1993.

Anglican Church

Anglican archdiocese project: "Women, the Church and Domestic/ Family Violence", 1991.

The Churches of Christ in Australia

The Pamphlet Club, a supplement to *The Australian Christian*, The Churches of Christ in Australia:
— Rosslyn Reed, "Resolving Domestic Violence: Conservative Christians and a Social Problem", in *The Pamphlet Club, op. cit.*, no. 361.
— Ranjini Rebera, "The Challenge to the Church", *op. cit.*, no. 364 (on church, patriarchy, feminism).
— Louis van Laar, "Violence within the Church", *op. cit.*, no. 370.

Articles in religious papers/journals

"Bring Violence out into the Open", in *The Advocate*, RCC, August 23, 1990 (on domestic violence within the church community).

"Ethics and the Minister", in *Australian Ministry*, February 1991.

Marjorie Lewis-Jones, "Sexual Violence in the Church", in *National Outlook*, an Australian Christian monthly, May 1991.

Tracy Hansen, "On Forgiving the Abuser — Is It Possible? Is It Necessary?", in *Priests and People*, vol. 5, no. 3, March 1991.

"What Does Violence against Women and Children Have to do with Christian Worship?", from a "Domestic Violence Resource Package" prepared by the Commission on the Status of Women, Australian Council of Churches, 1989/90 (focus on speaking the truth through prayer, symbol and ritual).

"Sexual Abuse within the Clergy", in *The Age*, Melbourne, July 1991.

Other

"Sanctity of Marriage Broken but not Her Faith", in *Canberra Times*, February 1991.

"Young Women Main Target in Sexual Harassment", in *Human Rights Newsletter*, Human Rights Commission, Canberra ACT, no. 12, February 1986.

"Information for People Responsible for Sexual Harassment in the Workplace", Human Rights Commission (includes a definition, suitable complaints, resolution and settlement procedures).

"How To Deal with a Complaint of Sexual Harassment", Trade Union Education Authority (includes a definition, grievance procedure, etc.).

"Sexual Harassment Module — Basic Delegates' Course", Human Rights Commission (information prepared for people delegated in the workplace to handle complaints of sexual harassment).

Canada

Uniting Church

Policy statement and principles and assumptions on sexual harassment as approved by the general executive, March 1985.

Theological statement, 1985: "Sexual Harassment Is a Sin".

"Sexual Harassment in the Church", Women in Ministry Committee, Division of Ministry Personnel & Education, Toronto, 1985.

Procedures for dealing with cases of sexual harassment, revised April 1990 (proposed by the UCC Division of Ministry Personnel & Education, with the intent and direction approved by the executive committee of the General Council).

Task force on abuse and harassment (in formation; will be responsible for gathering information about UCC policies on sexual harassment, evaluation of policies and action guidelines).

"Violence against Women", in *Women's Concerns*, fall 1990 (in memory of the 14 young women killed on the campus of the University of Montreal in December 1989).

Anglican Church

"Violence against Women", the report of the 1986 general synod (on abuse in society and church and proposals for change).

"Violence against Women: Why Are Women Victims of Men? What Must Be Changed?", April 1986 (response strategies for the church and recommendations to local congregations).

Procedures for dealing with cases of sexual harassment, revised April 1990.

Sexual abuse task force policies, December 12, 1990 (theological basis, principles, procedures).

Roman Catholic Church

Canadian Roman Catholic Bishops statement deploring violence against women: "Violence against women breaks the fifth commandment. It is a sin, a crime and a serious social problem. It is not only an individual, private or family matter."

Church-related

"Hands to End Violence against Women, a Resource for Congregational Use", Women's Inter-Church Council of Canada (WICC), Toronto, 1988 (case studies, suggestions for workshops, Bible studies, theological discussion, etc.).

"Wayward Priests To Get Counselling", in *Age*, April 6, 1988 (on psychological counselling for clerical paedophiles).

Other

"Violence against Women", in *Voices Rising*, vol. 4, no. 2 (a report on domestic violence in Argentina, Nicaragua).

Poster: "How Much Will the Child Resemble the Mother?", Ontario Medical Association.

Ghislan Laroche, "Harassment: The Hard Struggle of Bonnie Robichaud", in *Avenir*, February/March 1988 (on sexual harassment in the workplace).

"A Violent Legacy", in *Vis-à-Vis*, vol. 9, no. 2, a national newsletter on family violence, summer 1991 (six programmes that explore the links between child abuse and wife assault).

"Women Educating to End Violence against Women, Talking Feminist Popular Education", PERG, Canada, September 1992.

USA

Evangelical Lutheran Church in America

"Sexual Misconduct by Clergy within Pastoral Relationships", Northwest District of the American Lutheran Church working document, 1987.

Resolution on sexual harassment adopted by the 1989 ELCA churchwide assembly.

Sexual abuse and harassment: recommended elements of policy and procedures, January 1991.

Sexual abuse and harassment: definitions.

Presbyterian Church (USA)

Policy statement (on sexual harassment in the workplace).

Booklet: "Preventing Sexual Harassment".

Definition of sexual harassment.

Myths and acts about rape and battery.

Sexual harassment study, summary of findings, 1982.

Booklet: "Naming the Unnamed" (on sexual harassment in the church).

Booklet: "Violations against the Image of God, Exploitation of Women".

"A Time to Speak: Packet about Rape and Battery", the Council on Women and the Church.

Study/action guide for congregations: "Family Violence, a Religious Issue", 1988.

Policy regarding sexual misconduct by those involved in ministry, adopted by the Synod of the Rocky Mountains, October 27, 1990.

Recommended policy and procedures on sexual misconduct for congregations, employers, etc., April 1991.

"Presbyterian Bravery under Fire", in *Christianity and Crisis*, May 27, 1991 (on the refusal by an informal coalition of presbyters and synod executives to allow a two-year study and discussion of the report of the Presbyterians' Special Committee on Human Sexuality).

Jim Gittings, "A Bonfire in Baltimore", in *Christianity and Crisis*, *op. cit.* (on the committee report on human sexuality).

Karen Lebacqz, "Sex: Justice in Church and Society", in *Christianity and Crisis, op. cit.*

Episcopal Church

Booklet on sexual abuse of children: "Sarah", Office of Women in Ministry & Mission.

Handbook on domestic violence: "Breaking the Silence of Violence" (for clergy and religious counsellors, lay workers).

United Methodist Church

"Guidelines for Eliminating Racism, Ageism, Handicapism and Sexism", 1984 (on the use of language).

Sexual harassment policy for employers: reporting procedures, counselling, follow-up confidentiality, etc., 1988.

"Sexual Harassment in the United Methodist Church", November 1990 (extensive survey of laity, clergy, students, employees related to UMC "to determine the extent of sexual harassment and the policies and procedures to deal with it inside our church structures").

Resource package: "Ministries with Women in Crisis" (on physical violence, sexual abuse, economic exploitation, prison, pornography, prostitution, etc.).

"Crisis: Women's Experience and the Church's Response", final report of a UMC crisis survey, 1988-90.

Disciples of Christ

Booklet on domestic violence (challenges the churches to speak out).

Newsletter: "Working together to Prevent Sexual and Domestic Violence".

Guidelines on sexual contact by pastors and pastoral counsellors in professional relationships.

NCCC/USA

Policy statement on family violence and abuse: "The Church Must Be Willing to Call to Account those Persons and Institutions which Perpetuate Harm to Others".

American Friends Service Committee

Battered women information kit.

"Korean Immigrant Sues Employer for Harassment", in *Listen-RealLoud, News of Women's Liberation Worldwide*, vol. 6, no. 3, American Friends Service Committee, summer 1985.

United Church of Christ

"NH Church Faces up to Sexual Misconduct", and "Synod Delegates to Vote on Sexual Harassment Statement", in *United Church News*, April 1991.

Articles in religious papers/journals

Susan De Vogel Harrington, "Sexual Harassment in the Church", in *The Christian Ministry*, July/August 1988.

Susan Brooks, "Battered Women and the Bible", in *Christianity and Crisis*, November 1981.

Pamela Cooper-White, "Soul Stealing; Power Relations in Pastoral Sexual Abuse", in *The Christian Century*, February 20, 1991.

Marjorie Procter-Smith, "After Abuse Is Liturgy Possible?", in *Modern Liturgy*, vol. 18, no. 1.

Lindsay Hardin, "Clergy and Sexual Abuse", in *The Witness*, July/August 1990.

Judith Floyd, "To Greet Brothers without Fear: the Long Process of Healing after Rape", in *Sojourners*, February/March 1991.

Florence Rush, "Rape Victims still Victimized", in *New Directions for Women*, September/October 1987.

Marie Fortune, "Three Goals of Helpers in Sexual Abuse Situations", and "Steps in Justice Making after Abuse", for a workshop at the Centre for Christian Studies, March 1991.

Karen Lattea, "Ending the Stigma and the Silence", in *Sojourners*, July 1991.

"Clergy Sexual Abuse: A Justice Issue of the Church", in (Lutheran) *Vanguard*, May/June 1991.

Marie Fortune, "Confidentiality and Mandatory Reporting: A Clergy Dilemma?", in *Working Together*, vol. 6, no. 1.

"Institutional Violence: Women's Perspectives", *Miriam's Song V*, Priests For Equality, USA, 1992.

Other

"Sex Abuse Cases Rock the Clergy", in *Los Angeles Times*, August 3, 1990.

Marie Fortune, *Is Nothing Sacred? When Sex Invades the Pastoral Relationship*, Harper & Row, 1989.

Linda Hossie, "Experts Deplore Veil of Silence over Child Abuse", and "Youths Abused by Priests Called Victims of 'Seduction'", in *The Globe and Mail*, June 8, 1991.

Project on the status and education of women: "In Case of Sexual Harassment — A Guide for Women Students", Association of American Colleges, Washington D.C.

"How to Document Sexual Harassment in the Workplace", Working Women's Institute, USA, 1982.

"A Test of Two Exploratory Models of Women's Responses to Battery", in *Nursing Research*, February 1, 1989.

"Global Context of Violence at Home and on the Job", report of a consultation by UN/NGO Liaison, San Francisco, October 25, 1984.

Eldri Jauch, "Body Psychotherapy with Sexual Assault Survivors", Santa Barbara, California, USA, December 1987 (a research project which reviews the literature on the effects of rape and counselling with rape survivors as well as a brief review of body-mind approaches to psychotherapy).

Eldri Jauch, "Women against Rape", in *Tageszeitung*, May 8, 1991.

Charlotte Bunch, Roxanna Carrillo, "Gender Violence, A Development and Human Rights Issue", Centre For Women's Global Leadership, USA, 1991.

"Pornography Destroys", resource packet for an International Conference by the Religious Alliance against Pornography, 1993, USA.

"A Pattern of Rape, War Crimes in Bosnia", in *Newsweek*, January 11, 1993.

Latin America and Caribbean

Jamaica

"Child Sexual Abuse: An Issue of Male Power and Control", in *Sistren*, vol. 12, nos 2 & 3, Sistren Theatre Collective, Kingston, Jamaica, 1991.

Booklet: "'NO' to Sexual Violence", Sistren Theatre Collective, 1985.

Puerto Rico

Manual on sexual harassment in the workplace, Puerto Rican Institute for Civil Rights (PRICR) and PRISA with the help of the Caribbean Council of Churches, Bread for the World and others.

Public conferences on "Domestic violence" run by PRICR, at the United Methodist Church, San Juan, (November 13, 1990); at the UMC, Ponce (November 14, 1990); at the UMC, Hatillo (May 15, 1990); at the UMC, San Juan (November 16, 1990).

PRICR also supplies information about women's rights, domestic violence and spouse abuse, sex discrimination etc., makes referrals and selects cases for litigation on certain issues such as sexual harassment in the workplace.

"Day of International Solidarity; No more Violence against Women", in *Comai*, no. XIII, San Juan, November 1986. Complete report available from ISIS.

Brazil

"A Violência Doméstica", IDAC (Institute for Cultural Action), Rio de Janeiro, 1984 (on domestic violence).

"Sexual Violence against Women and Children", in *Conflitos de Terra*, vol. VI, 1986.

"When the Victim Is a Woman", Center for Study and Documentation for Community Action (CEDAC), in collaboration with the National Council for Women's Rights, and the Commission to Combat Violence, Sao Paulo, 1987 (a study of court cases and discriminatory legal treatment of women).

"The Domestic Worker", IDAC, Brazil, 1986.

"Brazil's Male 'Honour' Loses its Legitimacy", in *International Herald Tribune*, March 30, 1991 (on sexual violence in the family and rape).

"Criminal Injustice, Violence against Women in Brazil", Americas Watch Report, October 1991.

Dominican Republic

Mely Pappaterra, "Notes on Rape in the Dominican Republic", CIPAF, Santo Domingo, 1988.

Ecuador

Esly Regina Carvalho, booklet for International Women's Day, CLAI (Latin American Council of Churches).

Illustrated leaflets on sexual abuse of children, CLAI.

"Rape", a discussion paper produced by the Women's Assembly of Elda-Petrer.

"Sexual Violence", CAMVAC (support centre for women victims of rape).

Information leaflet on safe houses for women and children victims of domestic violence, Ministry of Social Welfare and Ecuador Centre for the Promotion and Action of Women.

Costa Rica

Vera Salles, "Violence against Women", in *Mujeres*, no. 20, July/August 1990, San Jose, Costa Rica (on sexual violence against women in police custody).

Paraguay

Information poster: "Violence against Women", 25 November Women's Collective, in *La Puerta de las Mujeres*, Paraguay, March 1991.

Peru

Booklet: "Sexual Siege in the Workplace", Peruvian Women's Centre Flora Tristan.

Mexico

The centre for the promotion of women workers (CAMT) seeks to inform women about their rights, human rights, labour laws, causes and possible solutions to the problems of rural women who seek work in towns: family disintegration, drugs, stress, domestic violence, sexual violence at home and in the workplace and sexual harassment in the streets.

"Gaining on Sexual Violence against Women", in *ListenReaLoud*, vol. 11, no. 1, 1991.

General

Report on the advisory group meeting on women, violence and the law, prepared by the Economic Commission for Latin America and the Caribbean, Caribbean Development and Cooperation Committee of the UN (describes the extent of sexual violence in Caribbean society and lists participants in the advisory group).

74

Africa

"Sexual Harassment: Report from Zimbabwe", in *Echo*, nos. 9-10, 1988.

"Report from Zimbabwe: Sexual Harassment", in *Sauti Ya Siti*, no. 5, March 1989.

"Rape: A Crime of Violence against Women", in *Manela*, vol. 1, no. 1, Zambia.

Jill Taylor and Sheelagh Stewart, "Sexual and Domestic Violence: Help, Recovery and Action in Zimbabwe", 1991.

"Violence against Women in Africa: A Human Rights Issue", in *African Woman*, no. 6, July-October 1992.

Shanta Bryant, "Women Rise up to Fight Rape," *All Africa Press Service*, January 20, 1992.

Asia

Lois Gehr, "A Christian Vision of Sexual Justice: Theological and Ethical Reflections on Violence against Women", in *In God's Image*, vol. 10, no. 1, Hong Kong, 1991.

Eunice Britto, "The Gajraula Incident" and other articles on rape in *In God's Image*, vol. 10, no. 2, Hong Kong, 1991.

"Women Fight against Sexual Discrimination at the Work Place", in *Asian Women Workers Newsletter*, vol. 10, no. 1, Hong Kong, March 1991.

"Sexual Harassment at Work: A Silenced Subject", in *Asian Women Workers Newsletter*, vol. 10, no. 2, Hong Kong, June 1991.

"Rape of her Privacy", "Break the Silence", and "Should the Woman Be Named?", in *WAVES*, AWAM (All Women's Action Society), Malaysia, May, 1991.

Action pack for campaign on legal reforms for women in Malaysia: "Violence against Women: Come together", AWAM (on domestic violence, women at work, women and family law, rape and sexual harassment, support for victims of rape).

"Indian Railways Women Workers Bear Harassment, Indignities", and "Sexual Harassment: Widespread but Ignored Job Hazard", in *Depthnews*, Manila, Philippines, September 1981.

"New Indian Law Boosts Campaign vs Wife-beaters", *Depthnews, op. cit.*, October 5, 1984.

"Rangoon Bars Waitresses in Restaurants", in *Depthnews*, January 26, 1984 (on absence of safeguards against sexual harassment).

Rokhsana Khondker, "Violence and Sexual Abuse", for the Centre for Advanced Studies. Paper on legal case studies in Bangladesh presented to the 4th International Interdisciplinary Congress on Women, Hunter College, New York City, June 1990 (complete report available from ISIS).

Rosella Camte-Bahni, "Wifebeating! Not a Hopeless Case", in *Igoroto* (an alternative women's magazine in the Cordilleras), vol. IV/1990, no. 4, Philippines.

Handbook: "Working with Rape Survivors", Women's Crisis Centre Network, Penang, Malaysia.

"Rape Victims Do Not Get Decent Legal Treatment", in *Bangkok Post*, August 22, 1990.

"Beyond Labour Issues: Women Workers in Asia", Committee for Asian Women (CAW), Hong Kong, 1988.

"Rape: Crime against All Women", and other articles on violence against women in *Documentation on Women's Concerns*, Library and Documentation Centre, All-India Association for Christian Higher Education, New Delhi, April 1991.

"Asian Women Seeking Wellness", in *ListenReaLoud*, vol. 11, no. 1, 1991.

Krishnaraj Maitreyi, ed., "Women and Violence: A Country Report", Research Centre for Women's Studies, SNDT Women's University, Bombay, 1991.

"Child Abuse", in *Verbatim*, no. 4, Centre for Development and Women's Studies, Madras, July-August 1992.

Posters and postcards: "Violence against Women, Creation and Humanity", Asia Pacific Forum on Women, Law and Development, Malaysia (part of a campaign in support of the attempt to bring rights of women to the centre of the UN 1993 World Conference on Human Rights, Vienna).

"Women's Rights, Human Rights", *Asia-Pacific Reflections*, APWLD, 1992.

"Pornography", Asian Women's Human Rights Commission, Philippines, 1991.

Pacific

"Battered Women", in *Ofis Blong Ol Meri Newsletter*, a project in cooperation with the World YWCA, June 1984.

"Domestic Violence", in *Women's Newsletter*, vol. 3, nos. 2 & 3, South Pacific Commission, Noumea, New Caledonia, April/July 1988.

"Women and the Law", in *PAWORNET Newsletter*, Pacific Regional YWCA Office, Suva, Fiji, December 8, 1991.

Videos: "Force Line" and "Women's Shame", Fiji women's movement, 1993 (case studies).

Middle East

Israel

Rape Crisis Centre information booklet, Tel Aviv.

Europe

General

"Freedom from Fear?", in *Change*, London, June 1986 (a survey and discussion of violence against women in various cultural and national contexts).

"European Women's Experiences in the Church", compiled by Musimbi Kanyoro from the proceedings of the European Women Theologians' Conference, Loccum, November 19-23, 1990, Lutheran World Federation.

"EC Code Proposed to Prevent Sexual Harassment", in *International Herald Tribune*, July 3, 1991.

Belgium

M. Smet (state secretary for social liberation), "Violence Solicited?", Brussels (on the circumstances, causes and consequences of sexual violence, for use by the police).

M. Smet, "First Aid for Use in Cases of Sexual Abuse of Children in Families".

Catrin Davies, "Free and Equal in Dignity and Rights? The Trafficking of Women to Europe", Quaker Council of European Affairs, August 1992.

Catrin Davies, "In the Darkest Corners... Women Enslaved in Europe", in *Around Europe*, no. 145, Quaker Council of European Affairs, June 1992.

Germany

Study on harassment, Ministry for Women, Bonn, reported in *Femina*, a supplement of the *Tribune de Genève*, April 12, 1991 (the first of its kind, the study showed that more than 70 percent of German women have been sexually harassed in the workplace).

"The Fear Is Always Present", in *Der Spiegel*, November 1991 (the figure of 8,000 cases of reported rape in Germany may be a gross underestimation; according to researchers at the Hamburg "Emergency number for women and girls victims of rape", at least 200,000 such cases occur, but go unreported).

"Most Working Women Are Victims of Sexual Harassment", in *Frankfurter Rundschau*, March 25, 1991 (according to a social research institute in Dortmund, 72 percent of working women have experienced such incidents).

Helga Lukoschat, "In the Healthy World of the DDR There Was no Physical Violence", in *Die Tageszeitung*, May 15, 1991.

"Violence, Decadematerialien, Evangelische Frauenhilfe in Westfalen e. V. (Westphalian Office, "Ecumenical Decade of Churches in Solidarity with Women"), December 1992.

Netherlands

"More Help from Pastors for Victims of Sexual Abuse", in *epd ZA* no. 130, July 10, 1991 (on special training for pastors to deal with sexual abuse or harassment cases within church structures, to be provided by the Dutch Reformed Churches).

France

"Femmes violées, humanité abusée, femmes et hommes dans l'Eglise", *Bulletin International*, no. 53, Paris, March 1993.

Switzerland

Viol Secours, a Geneva-based association of women working with victims of rape, has issued numerous publications on the causes of violence against women and the treatment of victims, including:
— "Myths about Rape, Sexual Harassment, and Women and the Law", March 1988.
— "Sexual Harassment: What Should Be Done?"
— "Incest Rape: Rapists in the Family", 1987.
— "Sexual Harassment in the Workplace: Enough!"
— "The Right to Work with Dignity. Sexual Harassment: An Abuse which Must Disappear", June 1991.
— "Against Rape and Violence Committed against Women", October 1988.

Other

"Sexual Harassment in the Workplace", no. 1, Swiss Trade Unions Federation, 1991.

Report on sexual abuse of children, in *Femina, op. cit.*, April 12, 1991.

"Wives Win Right to Say No", in *Evening Standard*, October 23, 1991 (on House of Lords ruling outlawing rape within marriage).

Flora Hunter and Patrick McGowan, "The End to 250 Years of Sexual Slavery", in *Evening Standard, op. cit.* (commentary on above-mentioned ruling).

"Rape in Marriage: Making this Crime Illegal", Women against Rape, King's Cross Women's Centre (commentary on above-mentioned ruling).

"I Said Nothing for Five Years", in *Tages-Anzeiger*, April 16, 1991 (a rape survivor describes her experience and its aftermath).

"Sexual Violence: The Rules of Power", in *Femmes suisses*, December 1989.

"Sexual Harassment before the Law", in *Femmes suisses*, August/September 1988.

"Maria's Honour Restored", in *Femmes suisses*, January 1990.

"Rape and Sexual Abuse : Torture and Ill-treatment of Women in Detention", Amnesty International, UK, December 1991.

"Freeing Ourselves from Violence", in *Women's World*, no. 26, ISIS/WICCE, winter 1991/92, Geneva, Switzerland.

"Violence against Women", in *Common Concern*, no. 77, March 1993, World YWCA, Geneva.

World Council of Churches

Report of conference on Women, Human Rights and Mission, Venice, Italy, June 24-30, 1979.

"Violence against Women and Sexual Harassment", in *Decade Link*, no. 8, May 1991.

"Slave Trade in Pakistan", in *Decade Link*, no. 11, August 1992.

"Churches Criticized for Silence on Child Violence", in *ibid*.

"La violence à l'encontre des femmes", in *ibid*.

"Sexual Abuse also Affects the Church", in *Assembly Line*, Canberra, February 18, 1991.

"When Christian Solidarity Is Broken", September 1991 (a pastoral/educational pamphlet in English, French, German and Spanish for use at ecumenical gatherings).

Aruna Gnanadason, "No Longer a Secret", in *One World*, October 1991.

Karen Granberg-Michaelson, "Violence against Women — Honesty in the Church", in *One World*, November 1991.

Rebecca Larson, "Violence against Women, Church, Women and Power", in *One World*, December 1991.

"Rape of Women in War — Report of an Ecumenical Women's Team Visit to Former Yugoslavia", December 1992.

United Nations

"Violence against Women in the Family", UN, New York, 1989.

Jan Martenson (under-secretary general for Human Rights), "Global Strategies for Achieving Gender Fairness in the Courts: Eliminating Violence against Women", UN Human Rights Commission, Geneva, February 5, 1992.

Lutheran World Federation

"Violence against Women", in *Women*, no. 32, July 1989 (articles by women from Europe, Australia, Asia, Pacific).

Cf. also Europe "Other" in this list.

World Alliance of Reformed Churches

"Prostitution of Children in Asia", in *WARC Update*, spring 1992.

Other

The Tribune, no. 46, International Women's Tribune Centre, New York, 1991 (issue on violence against women).

This list was compiled by the staff team on women, Unit III, Justice, Peace, Creation, World Council of Churches, Geneva).